# EVE
# Prayers

# MORNING
# Promises

## Understanding 12 Step Spirituality

edited by

Patrick J. Moriarty

Published by Glen Abbey Books, Inc.

Printed in the United States of America
Cover design by Michelle Ogata, WESDESIGN, Seattle, Washington

Library of Congress Cataloging in Publication Data

Evening prayers morning promises: understanding 12 step spirituality / edited by Patrick J. Moriarty
1. Alcoholics--Prayer--books and devotions--English.
I. Moriarty, Patrick J. II. Title: Understanding 12 step spirituality.
BL625.45.E9 1989 291.4'3--dc20 89-37966
ISBN: 0-934125-14-7

Disclaimer: The publication of this volume does not imply affiliation with nor approval or endorsement from Alcoholics Anonymous World Services, Inc.



Inquiries, orders, and catalog requests should be addressed to:

Glen Abbey Books, Inc.
P.O. Box 19762
Seattle, Washington 98109
Call toll-free (all U.S.) 1-800-782-2239

To

HENRIETTA S. THOMAS

# CONTENTS

# FOREWORD

Today finds many people concerned about their spiritual life. You hear people speak of their "spiritual program" or their "level of spirituality." What does all this mean? The whole concept of spirituality has taken on a world of different meanings. One can now go to spiritual healers like one goes to the dentist with a toothache. How does a person who is seeking to get started on a spiritual path actually begin?

*Evening Prayers Morning Promises* is about such a beginning. The author's journey takes us through the Twelve Steps of Alcoholics Anonymous. This guide through the Steps is conducted by one of A.A.'s many anonymous travelers. The author's story is chronicled according to his spiritual progress. The prayers and promises illuminate his interpretation of the spiritual characteristics of each Step. The quotations selected are as signposts, confirming the right direction.

Each prayer, promise, and reflection in this book is but a reminder of the fathomless depth of each Step. What you will gain from *Evening Prayers Morning Promises* is a new perspective on your own spirituality. Perhaps as a result you will find yourself reaching new levels of recovery in your Twelve Step journey. There is no right road to spiritual fulfillment. There is either your road or no road. This book will illuminate your road to spirituality. As you read, remember, go slow. Take your time. Read as if the light is in front of you, not behind. The prayers are for you, the promises are for your life.

I want to thank the author who shared so much of his life with me in the preparation of this book. He asked me to thank on his behalf all those travelers on the way to recovery who have so generously shared their light with him, and he asks that where you find light, you too might pass it on.

Patrick J. Moriarty

There is nothing I can give you which you have not; But there is much, very much that while I cannot give it, you can take.

No heaven can come to us unless our hearts find rest in today. Take heaven!

No peace lies in the future which is not hidden in this present instant. Take peace!

The gloom of the world is but a shadow behind it, yet within reach is joy.

There is radiance and glory in the darkness, could we but see, and to see, we have only to look. I beseech you to look.

Life is so generous a giver, but we, judging its gifts by their covering, cast them away as ugly, heavy or hard. Remove the covering, and you will find beneath it a living splendor, woven of love, by vision, with power.

Welcome it, grasp it and you touch the angel's hand that brings it to you. Everything we call a trial, a sorrow, or a duty, believe me, that angel's hand is there, the gift is there, and the wonder of an overshadowing presence.

Our joys too, be not content with them as joys. They too, conceal livening gifts.

And so this time I greet you, not quite as the world sends greetings but with profound esteem and with the prayer that for you now and forever, the day breaks, and the shadows flee.

A Christmas card by Fra Giovanni, 1513 A.D.

# STEP ONE

We admitted we were powerless over alcohol - that our lives had become unmanageable.

## Evening Prayers and Reflections for Revelation

## Morning Promises and Reflections of Fortitude

## Evening Prayer 1:1

*What is called a reason for living is also an excellent reason for dying.*
*Albert Camus*

**O Mysterious One,** I do not know how to address You. Show me the way through the darkness. All I feel is fear; all I know is nothing works; all I am aware of is my own abyss. I exist only to find some way out. I cannot help myself. I know no power that can free me from my own life. I present myself before that which I know only by reputation, by the words of others. Please take this death of mine and create life. Amen.

*In the midst of life is death.*
*The Book of Common Prayer*

## Evening Reflection 1:1

*Healthy children will not fear life if their elders have integrity enough not to fear death.*
*Eric H. Erickson*

On a rainy fall night in 1979 in Washington D.C., my despair was deep. I was comforting myself in my favorite bar near Capitol Hill, The Irish Times. There I found men and women like myself, exiles from the sixties who shared a common frustration with the direction of their lives.

I had worked with the poor for the entire decade of the 1970's. The non-profit group I represented made many valiant attempts at bettering the social and economic conditions of poor communities. Time and again those efforts were cancelled out by new problems or unseen old problems.

My good deeds over the years had earned me a barstool of great distinction at The Irish Times. How I enjoyed myself during the years at that bar! Here we shared victories and planned work. We were God's little helpers, aligned with the forces of good, fighting the forces of evil, poor against rich. I was Robin Hood.

That evening I met a lovely Irish entertainer. We seemed to have a lot in common: we both liked to wash down our Irish whiskey with pints of Harp. We entertained each other for hours. She would sing and drink, I would applaud and drink, and together we would attempt conversation.

Very little of that was possible as the evening wore on.

At midnight, both drunk, we decided it was time to leave. Three men appeared from an alleyway, and blocked our path. One of the men moved toward the woman and spun her around. The other two converged on me. I clenched my fists and took a stance that said I was prepared to hold my ground, adrenaline pumping through me at an awful rate. I felt like a cornered rat. One of the men pawed at the woman and dragged her into the alleyway. I heard a clarion call to attack. I surged ahead, flailing at my two opponents. I felt nothing but the fury of a wild man. This was war. I kicked one man so hard I heard his leg break. He went down. The other two came at me. The woman ran off into the night. I engaged one man in an old fashioned fist fight. The other disappeared. He came back with their car and a tire iron. He hammered my face with the tire iron. I went down, out cold.

The police later told me that the men got into their car and drove it over me to make it appear I was a hit and run victim. My rib cage collapsed and lacerated all my internal organs. Many bones were broken.

The men then packed my carcass into their car, drove a mile or so and tossed me over a freeway overpass to the ground 30 feet below. There I lay, comatose, bleeding internally, dying.

I had always been skeptical of people who claimed out-of-body experiences. Yet as I lay dying, I moved out of my body. I saw myself lying utterly still. I was terrified. I could not die in this state. Something was desperately wrong. I had to find help. A revelation was just beginning for me.

*All our life is but going out to the place of execution, to death.*
*John Donne*

## Evening Prayer 1:2

*One wants to live, of course, indeed one only stays alive by virtue of the fear of death.*
*George Orwell*

**O Thou Who Is Known As Father**, can You ever love me? A man who has sunk so low, who is known only by his scars, and those he has administered to others? I admit that if there is a living end, I am there. I admit that life has become unmanageable. I cannot go on without help. I must believe that there is a Power greater than myself. I scream to Thee to show Thyself... now. Amen.

*A dead man is nothing more than a dead man, and a living man of the slightest pretensions is stronger than the dead man's memory.*
*Napoleon I*

## Evening Reflection 1:2

*It matters not how man dies but how he lives. The act of dying is not of importance, it lasts so short a time.*
*Samuel Johnson*

My spirit moved up the embankment to the road and waited for a passing car. I cried out for help. None came. I looked down at my body and knew I must return. I re-entered myself. After a long time, I re-enacted the same scene, once again to no avail. Again I returned to my body.

Shortly before daybreak, I emerged one more time. How I was surviving all this, I do not know. I suspect that I was dying and coming back. This time I found a police patrol car. I instructed them as to the whereabouts of my body. They drove to where I was and found a corpse.

Half way to the morgue, I began to show signs of life. I was quickly taken to the trauma unit of the Washington D.C. Hospital Center. The doctors put me on a life support system while they attempted to correct some of the damage done to me.

I am told I was in the operating room most of a day, and in the recovery room for two. My body continued to fight the instinct to die. My spirit continued to wage battle to live, knowing that the appointed hour had not come.

When I regained consciousness, there was a small group of people huddled around my bed: a priest, a policeman, a nun, nurses and my two brothers. I remember ever so faintly a person touching my head with some kind of liquid. The priest was administering the last rites. The nun leaned over me to wipe my face.

I asked her, "What am I to do?" Without hesitation, she answered, "Follow the light. Go to where the light goes. If the light goes right, follow the light right. If it goes left, follow the light left. Keep following the light."

I could see no light. I was going to find no relief from my pain in death. The priest, having completed the sacrament, leaned over me and asked, "Is there anything you want from me?" He was asking if it were my intention to make my last confession. I looked up at him and said, "Yes, Father - could you bring me a pint of vodka?"

At that moment I realized I was powerless over alcohol. My last wish was, "Get me a pint of vodka."

*That whole motley confusion of acts, omissions, regrets and hopes which is the life of each one of us finds in death, not meaning or explanation, but an end.*
*Octavio Paz*

## Evening Prayer 1:3

*Some people seem to think that death is the only reality in life. Others, happier and rightlier minded, see and feel that life is the true reality in death.*
*Julius Charles Hare*

**O Thou Nameless One**, to whom I come broken, weak and helplessly alone, I know not where to go nor what to do. The pain I feel scours my body, thrashes my heart, and sours my mind. I admit my defeat. I cannot manage my life. I cannot manage my death. Accept this admission as my absolute resignation from the struggle to claim personal victory over my life. I realize that if there be such a Power, that Power does not come from me. I will await Your strength, but please come quickly. Amen.

*Life and death is cat and dog in this double bed of a world.*
*Christopher Fry*

## Evening Reflection 1:3

*Grieve not; though the journey of life be bitter, and the end unseen, there is no road which does not lead to an end.*
*Hafiz*

I lay three months confined to bed, my jaws wired shut, contemplating the fact that I could not live without liquor and I could not die without liquor. Every other reality in my life was subjected to this all-determining fact, the revelation of my powerlessness over alcohol. I tried to regain a foothold on life and come up with a logical explanation for the prior events. None came.

I asked the police if they remembered me coming to them for help. They insisted that no one came to them. They just found themselves rather aimlessly travelling to that remote spot. They elected to park underneath the overpass for no apparent reason. Absolutely nothing made sense. The only clear picture I got from the events of that night was that I was powerless over alcohol.

Revelation for me was a split second of truth about myself that managed to penetrate my arsenal of defense. I would surely die if I did not stop drinking. Living, I would continue to live in hell. There was no exit from my pain. I saw through to the tragic conclusion of my life.

I was burned by this truth, by the white hot heat of its message. I had to remove myself from the heat or allow myself to be burned up. But how could I move away?

The revelation that I was sick unto death, that the hell I experienced would never leave me, was as stark a happening as a man or woman will ever have. If I elected to walk with this reality, I brought many with me. The havoc that I wreaked in my drinking would continue. I would bring down all the people, places, and things that I held dear. The tragic march through Hell would destroy everything.

*The whole life of instinct serves the one end of bringing about death.*
*Sigmund Freud*

## Evening Prayer 1:4

*There is silence that saith, "Ask me!" There is silence that nothing saith; One is the silence of life forlorn, One is, and the other shall be.*
*Christina Rossetti*

**O Thou Whom I Vaguely Remember As God,** I give to Thee the sum and substance of my life. It has been revealed to me that if my life remains in my hands, all is lost. I stop now. I shall go no further. If there is any relief from my out-of-control life, it will come from the vague force identified as God. Come now, come quickly, come alone. Amen.

*Death then, being the way and condition of life, we cannot love to live if we cannot bear to die.*
*William Penn*

## Evening Reflection 1:4

*The weariest and most loathed worldly life that age, ache, penury, and imprisonment can lay on nature is a paradise to what we fear of death.*
*Shakespeare*

The revelation of the true condition of an alcoholic can also lead to an admission of utter defeat. The disease had destroyed me, but I was not dead. The revelation, while disclosing such unrelentingly painful truth, also revealed a way out. The path is simple, clear and well travelled. The path away from the heat of the living hell is being on a Twelve-Step Program. The revelation is that the end is the beginning and the beginning is the end.

A paradox? Yes. I am dealing with realities discovered in a spiritual dimension. Logic and reason are only marginally helpful. The First Step revelation is that in admitting defeat and utter powerlessness over alcohol, I can finally begin to live. The spiritual force of this revelation is overpowering. I now have admitted to the existence of a universe that, in at least one instance, is more powerful than I am. Alcohol, a man-made commodity with no life of its own, has a power and force that, when consumed, transforms everyone and everything that it touches. The revelation of powerlessness over this force is the beginning of spirituality.

The First Step is my hearing the revelation that was sent to me, simply hearing the words and allowing them to seep into my consciousness. This allows the idol that I have made of my own powers to collapse. What I heard from my hospital bed was "Let Go, Let God." Submit to my powerlessness; become totally, irrevocably defeated; do not lift one finger to defend myself. Let it be over.

*Death is but an instant, life a long torment.*
*Bernard Joseph Saurin*

## Morning Promise 1:1

*People are too durable, that's their main trouble. They can do too much to themselves, they last too long.*
*Bertolt Brecht*

I hear myself say, "Live and let live. One step at a time. Think, think, think. First things first." Where do these words come from? What power they have over me! What strength they give me! I hear their meaning. They move me. I know not why - yet I continue to say, "Yes! Yes! Yes!"

*Like strength is felt from hope, and from despair.*
*Homer*

## Morning Reflection 1:1

*He who has calmly reconciled his life to fate, and set proud death beneath his feet, can look fortune in the face, unbending both to good and bad: his countenance unconquered he can show.*
*Boethius*

The spiritual promise that emanates from the Prayer of Revelation is that I will have fortitude. I will have strength given to me from a source outside myself, present whenever I ask. I cannot own the strength. I only borrow the power while I need it. Then, as someone comes to me and asks to use the strength, I pass it on.

There exists for me only enough strength to get me through one day. There is no such thing as a year's worth. I cannot borrow strength two years down the road. I can ask for and use only that which is allotted for the particular day I am living.

My physical wounds healed. My broken bones, my lacerated organs, skull fracture, shattered pelvis, collapsed lung--all were better. Days became weeks and weeks months. I had nothing to drink. My mentor let me know that I must stay rooted on the First Step, that I must never forget that I was, I am, and I will continue to be powerless over the first drink.

The test came on my way to the store for a newspaper and some fresh fruit. As I turned the corner, I walked by a sign, Kelly's Tavern. I was pulled into the door. I walked over to the bar. The bartender was serving a customer and had his back to me.

I turned and faced the juke box. At that moment a new song began to play. "When you walk through the night, hold your head up high and don't be afraid of the dark... walk on, walk on with hope in your heart and you'll never walk alone."

My life stopped at that moment. My feet moved to the door. My hand grasped the doorknob and I moved through the door. I was outside. I was free. The power that was not from me allowed me to borrow it for a moment. I was given fortitude.

*To bear is to conquer our fate.*
*Thomas Campbell*

## Morning Promise 1:2

*The bitter and the sweet come from the outside, the hard from within, from one's own efforts.*
*Einstein*

Day after day the promise of fortitude is realized. The unnamed unknown Power continues to walk with me. Why does this Power stay with me? What have I ever done to deserve such loyal support? Have I not spent most of my life cursing It? I am embarrassed to say that I do not know how to pray. I do not know how to talk with the Unknown. I can only say thank you for this day.

*They that sow in tears shall reap in joy.*
*Bible*

## Morning Reflection 1:2

*He that would have the fruit must climb the tree.*
*Thomas Fuller*

A revelation can be a most mundane experience. My friend Jack recounts such a moment.

On a certain Friday, he was itching for a drink. He attended a meeting, but said nothing and heard less. He had not been reaching out to take his allotment of strength in those all-important after-meeting coffee sessions.

He realized that he had to attend another meeting or he would relinquish himself to the power of alcohol. He went to a meeting in skid row. The men and women who sat around the tables had been brutalized by the bottle. The rapacious creditor that is alcohol had extracted heavy penalties from them.

Jack sat down with a cup of coffee. His hands trembled. He could hardly see through the sweat that poured down his face. He began to pant. His pulse quickened. Just as he was about to bolt from the meeting hall and run to a liquor store, an old Indian man sat down next to him.

The Indian was huge, maybe 6'6" and 280 pounds. His face was wrinkled in a way that said he had slept a night or two underneath a bridge. He wrapped his huge hand around Jack's and said, "Son, I want to remind you that we do this program one day at a time. Whatever it is that is going on in you, you are going to get through it. It will pass. Your day is almost over. Take real good care." He gave Jack's hand a gentle squeeze and was gone.

*Try first thyself, and after call in God; for to the worker God himself lends all.*
*Hippolytus*

## Morning Promise 1:3

*We seldom break our leg so long as life continues a toilsome upward climb. The danger comes when we begin to take things easily and choose the convenient paths.*
*Nietzsche*

I never thought I would appreciate the morning, the rain, being alone, empty pockets, dirty socks, warm pop. I never thought I would actually look forward to being with people who do not drink, do drugs, or alter their reality. I find myself living with questions rather than insisting on knowing answers. I find myself talking, sharing, weeping, laughing and wondrously sleeping. Sleeping deeply, dreaming and being refreshed by the morning.

*He who limps is still walking.*
*Stanislaw Lec*

## Morning Reflection 1:3

*To travel hopefully is a better thing than to arrive, and the true success is to labor.*
*Robert Louis Stevenson*

Jack felt the air flow out of his body. The tension was released. His heart slowed down. He stopped shaking and sweating. His eyes filled with tears. He began to cry softly. He had received fortitude. He knew that this day would pass without his taking a drink. He had won because the old Indian had won and the old Indian had won because the program had won.

The message was being carried, a gigantic global circle of people passing one another bits of fortitude and hope. This emissary saved Jack's life and gave him permission to join the human race. He had always needed people but never had he asked for help. He had always wanted to be strengthened by another, but could never reach out and accept it when it was offered. The Indian gave him the gift to receive the promise of his revelation. There would be fortitude to live as one powerless over alcohol.

*Nothing can come of nothing.*
*Shakespeare*

## Morning Promise 1:4

*Instead of complaining that God had hidden Himself, you will give Him thanks for having revealed so much of Himself.*
*Pascal*

I am promised fortitude. I am promised strength. I am promised life for one more day. I do not have to look to myself, my addiction, or to anything I have ever looked to before for strength. I am promised that somehow, some way, from some unknown source, a Power will emerge with the strength to live one more day.

*The ultimate gift of conscious life is a sense of the mystery that encompasses it.*
*Lewis Mumford*

## Morning Reflection 1:4

*If I were to begin life again, I should want it what it was. I would only open my eyes a little more.*
*Jules Renard*

I am prone to forget about my fortitude. There are days when I feel so good I believe strength is no longer needed. I have used all the fortitude that I need and I will not ask for help this day.

The end result is always the same. As I take more control over life, the more powerless I become over the outcome of my life.

I must remember the promise that I have as a result of my revelation is that I have enough fortitude for each and every single day. I must collect each day's fortitude. To understand the true nature of fortitude, I must first understand from where it comes.

Fortitude is not a state of mind. I don't make myself strong by thinking about being strong. Nor is fortitude the result of a courageous heart. A strong heart will help me run a marathon, but will not be an adequate defense against alcohol. Fortitude is a gift that I can rely on but cannot possess. It comes from sources outside myself.

This is the reason why people who have had a similar revelation about their powerlessness need to congregate together and share their fortitude, their hope, and their experience. It is through just such sharing that fortitude is passed around, each person borrowing from each other.

Don't be surprised when someone takes strength from you. You'll be amazed with yourself. You'll wonder where that bit of fortitude came from. You never knew you had it.

*If thou tellest the sorrows of thy heart, let it be to him in whose countenance thou mayst be assured of prompt consolation.*
*Sa'di*

# STEP TWO

Came to believe that a Power greater than ourselves could restore us to sanity.

## Evening Prayers and Reflections for Belief

## Morning Promises and Reflections of Truth

## Evening Prayer 2:1

*He does not believe that does not live according to his belief.*
*Thomas Fuller*

**O Nameless One**, to whom I come with fear and trepidation, I ask You for the presence of mind, body, and spirit to accept the saving strength that awaits me each day. Let me this day keep my eyes alert, my heart open, and my spirit poised so I seize every opportunity to believe. Today I am weak, I am afraid, I am ashamed. I feel sick and loveless. I am a stranger in a strange land, homeless, a refugee. I have used up all my own power. I ask for Your help. Let Your presence stay in my life. Amen.

*Man is a credulous animal, and must believe sometime; in the absence of good grounds for belief, he will be satisfied with bad ones.*
*Bertrand Russell*

## Evening Reflection 2:1

*Where there is no hope there can be no endeavour.*
*Samuel Johnson*

My spiritual condition during alcoholic insanity was frozen solid. There was nothing, save the divine revelation, that could penetrate my shell of isolation. The spirituality of Step One is a blessing of consciousness. Prior to my revelation of powerlessness, I claimed authorship of my own universe. I brought all this misery on myself. Now, after the revelation, I have come to see alcohol has always had power over me.

I must remember not all spiritual states of being are in the form of electric shocks to the soul. My belief in a Power greater than myself is one that I will develop over time. It is tied to my new-found sanity.

My restoration to sanity is like the restoration of an old building, brick by brick, cornice by cornice. The spiritual point of Step Two is, in believing, I am given all that I need to begin getting sane. The very act of believing insures my sanity.

I soon learn all believers are not the same. Some believe more deeply than others, are more reliant on their Higher Power. Newcomers to the business of believing are less reliant. I should always be moving toward a deeper reliance on God's Power.

Sanity does not mean I am given rational answers for all things that befall me. I am not given boxes in which to put all events of my life. The world is not rational; why should sanity impose something that is not there? Sanity does not mean I will be tuned into the essential fairness of people, places, and things. No such luck. Sanity cannot give me something which doesn't exist.

Insanity is living in a make-believe world. My excuse for living a make-believe existence is that I think I can live in no other world. Sanity is being delivered to the truth: yes, I can live in the world as it is. Sanity doesn't change the world; it changes my relationship to the world.

*We are so constituted that we believe the most incredible things; and, once they are engraved upon the memory, woe to him who would endeavor to erase them.*
*Goethe*

## Evening Prayer 2:2

*The darkness of night, like pain, is dumb, the darkness of dawn, like peace, is silent.*
*Rabindranath Tagore*

**O That In Whom All Things Make Sense,** I ask to believe I no longer have to run from life. I can react to the events of this day as a normal person. I can have normal feelings. I can feel joy and sadness. I live the promise that the running is over, the hiding behind me. The masks have come off. I promise to remember that I am not the creator of this sanity. I am but the recipient of a gift from a Power that is greater than me. I shall not forget the torment of the insane life. I give thanks and rejoice in this day. I breathe deeply, fully and freely. Thank you. Amen.

*When water covers the head, a hundred fathoms are as one.*
*Persian Proverb*

## Evening Reflection 2:2

*In darkness one may be ashamed of what one does, without the shame of disgrace.*
*Sophocles*

Sanity seems like an ancient memory. For me, it has been decades since I felt safe and secure. My belly has been in constant upheaval during my drinking career. My nervous system is starved without alcohol. Time away from the bottle throws me into an anxious frenzy. How long has it been since I had several nights together of deep, healing, sound sleep?

The memory of waking in the middle of the night in a sweating frenzy is worn like a stigma. That mad feeling that had me reaching for tranquilizers or some other sedative is still a burning reality. The awful recognition that I could not fully account for my behavior after my first drink is the truth about my drinking.

The feeling of insanity is perhaps the worst of all human experiences: the emotion of abject terror; the death that does not kill; the fire that burns but does not consume; the darkness that does not lift; the loneliness that is constant; the feeling that I have been banished to a world where there is no joy, a perpetual stranger who has been rejected from all circles of friendship. I tell myself that I deserve no love and am incapable of giving love, and therefore will live in a world devoid of love.

*The mass of men lead lives of quiet desperation. What is called resignation is confirmed desperation. From the desperate city you go into the desperate country, and have to console yourself with the bravery of minks and muskrats.*
*Thoreau*

## Evening Prayer 2:3

*Whenever the weak make an alliance with the strong, they are the strong's dependents.*
*Walter Savage Landor*

**O That Which I Have Denied A Thousand Times,** I have tried to believe in something. I have sought to believe in relationships. I have believed in nature. I have read books on great things, held firmly to ideas that I perceived as enormously important. I have sought belief in every corner but with You. I have run from You and run hard. Oh Nameless One, I have stopped running. I turn at this moment to You and the promise of belief. Take me. Take me now. Amen.

*There is nothing so imperious as feebleness which feels itself supported by force.*
*Napoleon I*

## Evening Reflection 2:3

*The weakest and most timorous are the most revengeful and implacable.*
*Thomas Fuller*

My battles with the truth took me deep into my fears. My fear of heights was becoming a real problem for me. It got worse when I drank the night before a trip. I would be very jittery in the morning. Then I would have to squeeze myself on a crowded airplane and fly at 36,000 feet. It became intolerable when I could not get my hands on a Screwdriver or a Bloody Mary. I began packing booze in my briefcase so I would have it close by.

The dramatic crack in my armor came one morning in Chicago. I had worked for months on a piece of legislation for the Trust Territory of the Pacific. The bill would provide $2 million for an economic and social development program. The leadership of the Islands came to Washington D.C. to testify.

We rolled out the red carpet for the three leaders. They came to Chicago and met with our staff there. Since I was lead person on this project, it became my job to provide a tour of the city. Remember, these men were tribal leaders. None of them had spent much time off remote atolls in the middle of the Pacific. They had never seen a city the size of Chicago.

The night before we were to leave on our trip through the city, I drank a quart of vodka with a woman I was seeing at the time. I got about three hours of sleep before I was to breakfast with them in their downtown hotel. They insisted on having breakfast on the deck fifty stories up, so they could then take in the beautiful view. I had no choice but to agree.

There was no booze to calm my nerves. At this point I had not yet learned about tranquilizers. My head became light. My eyes focused on the rail surrounding the deck. Fascination with the guard rail overpowered me. I could hardly resist the temptation to run and leap over. I wanted to ask the waiter to get a chain and lock me into my chair. I could not eat my food. I was dizzy, nauseous, completely out of control. It seemed obvious to me I would die at any moment.

*He is a fool who tries to match his strength with the stronger. He will lose his battle, and with the shame will be hurt also.*
*Hesiod*

## Evening Prayer 2:4

*In tragedy every moment is eternity; in comedy, eternity is a moment.*
*Christopher Fry*

**O Great Stranger**, whom I have met at the end of a long lonely road in the middle of the night, You have come when I was unable to go one more inch, when everyone I had ever loved had abandoned me, when my pockets were empty and my body bruised and scarred. You offer me the reassurance of new life. I must now surrender, completely, totally, utterly without condition. I have lost the battle and won the war. Amen.

*One cannot balance tragedy in the scales unless one weighs it with the tragic heart.*
*Stephen Vincent Benet*

## Evening Reflection 2:4

*A tragic situation exists precisely when virtue does not triumph but when it is still felt that man is nobler than the forces which destroy him.*
*George Orwell*

The prayer of the Second Step is for belief in a Power greater than myself, that can restore me to sanity. A belief does not come from the same source of knowledge as rationality. I can't think my way into belief.

Beliefs and truths well up from a much deeper level of understanding. There are times when I hear something and I just know that it is true.

I may not have all the facts before me, but I feel the truth in my toes. There are occasions when I come into the presence of a person and know that this person is not good for me. Some people call this a sixth sense or intuition. I suspect that using this power is difficult because I have had so little practice. I must get instruction in this spiritual practice by watching others, attending my 12 Step meetings and talking with those who live their belief.

Belief is a spiritual state before it is an idea. I am sober today. I am an alcoholic. How can these two statements be true at precisely the same time? The only explanation is that a Power greater than the alcoholic is keeping this alcoholic sober. I believe in that Power because It is working right now in me.

*My barstool talk was no longer animated, dreaming about the future, but rather despairing babble about what may befall us. Alcohol was no longer fueling the laughter; it was now drowning the tears.*
*Patrick Moriarty*

## Morning Promise 2:1

*Truth seems to come with its final word; and the final word gives birth to its next.*
*Rabindranath Tagore*

The truth for me has been like a prism that continuously changes colors with light's reflection. I have come to a point where I have ceased to understand. I cannot remember whether to walk when the light turns green or red. I forget what I did the night before. I cannot distinguish friend from foe. I hear voices from rocks and trees. The promise of truth is like being given a compass. Finally the world stops spinning and I am given an anchor to root my life. The Power that I can trust believes in me, as long as I do not believe in me.

*Truth exists. Only lies are invented.*
*Georges Braque*

## Morning Reflection 2:1

*Truth is tough. It will not break, like a bubble, at a touch; nay, you may kick it about all day like a football, and it will be round and full at evening.*
*Oliver Wendell Holmes, Sr.*

Step Two says I will "come to believe." I am not returning to an old belief system. This belief is about being restored to sanity, no more, no less. I came to believe by watching others act sane. Some of these people handle situations with sanity and reasonableness that shocks me. This is the essence of the miracle of 12 Step recovery groups. One miracle begets another - one person's sanity is translated into another 24 hours.

The Second Step promise of truth means I can begin a love affair with reality. A sponsor properly used can show how this love affair is carried on. Situations that would formerly baffle me and over which I would drink, become an insignificant moment in the day.

At first, it was incomprehensible to me that truth does not kill. I find it difficult to believe the truth will set me free. I must use wise guides through this jungle of deceptions. I am becoming a person who is not afraid of having my hand held. I have not been asked at this point to turn my will and my life over to God. I have only been asked to believe that something could make me sane again.

I know there is something that has made my life miserable, and it is entirely outside my ability to control. In my revelations of powerlessness I had my mind and heart pried open just a bit. I must use the new found openmindedness to go just a bit further.

The promise of truthfulness can be witnessed each day in the life of my sponsor. He can come to embody the essence of a higher power. As I watch this person live an alcohol- and drug-free life, I begin to imagine myself in his shoes. After a few days, weeks, or months of walking in lock step behind my sponsor, I too discover that I have been walking with the truth. Reality has not mowed me down. A Power greater than I is doing that which I could not do for myself. Now I am ready to turn my will and my life over to that power.

*Lies are the religion of slaves and bosses. Truth is the god of the free man.*
*Maxim Gorky*

## Morning Promise 2:2

*A quiet conscience sleeps in thunder.*
*English Proverb*

I cannot remember a time when truth was not an issue. After I stopped going to confession, I lost accountability to a Higher Power. Truth and honesty soured in me like spoiled milk. Issues like success, power and influence became more important than abstract virtues like truth. Yet every time I shaded a story to suit my own purposes, acid would be released from my stomach and I felt the lie. Truth is like warm milk. Truth is like perfect pitch. Truth is like a firm handshake. Truth is like a clear head in the morning. Truth is never having to look over your shoulder. Truth is communion with God.

*A state of conscience is higher than a state of innocence.*
*Thomas Mann*

## Morning Reflection 2:2

*Conscience is the guardian in the individual of the rules which the community has evolved for its own preservation.*
*W. Somerset Maugham*

I remember developing a phobia about bridges. Whenever I crossed a bridge, I was afraid an urge might come over me to leap out of my car and fling myself over the rail. Each year the fear became a little worse.

One afternoon while I was in San Francisco, a group of us decided to stroll across the Golden Gate Bridge. I got halfway across before I panicked. I couldn't keep myself from running to the other side. I realized that my fear was now a full blown phobia. Rather than confront my fear, I told myself to keep off bridges.

I travelled a great deal and made sure I had several drinks before boarding a flight. Drinking seemed to calm me down, so I identified booze as the solution rather than the problem. When I stayed in a hotel, I pleaded for a room on a lower floor. I became critically aware of how much we are off the ground in this world of ours.

Insanity is not a clinical trade name for depression; it is the total loss of touch with reality. Sane people do not cross bridges and expect to jump. Sane people do not forget how to breathe.

Insanity for most alcoholics is the fact of being captured by abject fear. A power that can restore sanity is without question my single greatest all-consuming prayer. If hell has a face in this world, it is the face of my insane fear.

The promise that comes from believing is living the truth. The life I have been given to live is not bad, not essentially different from any other life. I no longer must adjust reality with chemicals to survive. The truth is good. It is sometimes hard, sometimes sad, but always right. Truth will not hurt me. The truth about life is not my invention because I am not God.

Truth is God's way of revealing His will. If I am true to life I will be true to myself. I will participate in the natural balance that exists between people, places, and things. I find myself respecting the truth as others may see it. I no longer insist on having everything my way. I am more respectful of the environment, more respectful of the rights and priorities of other people.

*A good conscience is the best divinity.*
*Thomas Fuller*

## Morning Promise 2:3

*In a real dark night of the soul it is always three o'clock in the morning, day after day.*
*F. Scott Fitzgerald*

Why is it that precisely when things seem their bleakest I have my most glorious moments? Why is it that in the work of the Spirit everything seems so contradictory? Up is down, right is left. Maybe everything is right, and I am the only one that is upside down, inside out. I realize that the only way I ever really get to the truth is to run out of rope. When I quit putting my hope in all manner of things, I receive hope. This fact I can trust now and forever.

*In despair there are the most intense enjoyments, especially when one is very acutely conscious of the hopelessness of one's position.*
*Dostoevsky*

## Morning Reflection 2:3

*There's something so showy about desperation, it takes hard wits to see it's a grandiose form of funk.*
*Elizabeth Bowen*

The truth was cracking me up. After half an hour at fifty stories, I began to panic. My breathing was so heavy you would have thought I'd walked up all fifty flights of stairs. The more air I took in, the more air I felt I needed.

The three visitors from the Marshall Islands did not know what to make of it. They called room service and had the bellman bring me water. When he arrived, I was pacing around the deck like a caged lion, sucking air as if I were trapped in an oxygen-less cave. The bellman asked me if I was having a heart attack. That was it, yes, indeed; I was 26 years old and I was having a heart attack.

Rather than asking the bellman to call a cab or an ambulance, I asked my Island friends to drive me to the hospital. I was gasping like a madman by the time we reached the car. We got in, and discovered no one but me could drive. So I crawled into the driver's seat, and with my head hanging out the window, drove myself to the emergency entrance of Bethany Brethren Hospital.

I stumbled in and announced to the nurse I was having a heart attack. She immediately got the trauma team assembled and put me on oxygen. After awhile, a doctor checked my vitals, my heartbeat, and the life support monitors. He then turned to the head nurse and told her to give me 20 milligrams of Valium. In a short time I felt normal. They moved me up to another room to conduct further examinations. I, of course, begged for more Valium. After the tests, it was quite clear that I had not had a heart attack.

I went to sleep and woke up in the middle of the night. I rang for the nurse to bring me more Valium. A tough-looking woman answered my call. She had no Valium with her. She told me she knew what my problem was. With great interest, I asked, "What is it?" She answered, "Boy, you are an alcoholic. You had a panic attack. You're killing yourself with that booze. We can calm you down with pills, but that won't solve your problem." Those words cut me to the quick. You Are An Alcoholic. I could have added the observation that I was also insane. The alcohol was not curtailing my madness; it was creating it.

*To eat bread without hope is still slowly to starve to death.*
*Pearl S. Buck*

# Morning Promise 2:4

*Conscience does make cowards of us all.*
*Shakespeare*

My uncle was the kind of man who liked to play games with young children. He would hold a peanut in one hand and ask you to guess which hand it was in. Needless to say, the peanut was always in the other hand. It seemed like every human being I met after Uncle Paul always had the peanut in the other hand. I became Uncle Paul somewhere down the line, except I never had a peanut. Now I can believe in a Higher Power that will never trick me. I can believe that if I stay close to this Force, I will be safe. I will always find the hand with the peanut.

*A peace above all earthly dignities, a still and quiet conscience.*
*Shakespeare*

## Morning Reflection 2:4

*The glory of good men is in their conscience and not in the mouths of men.*
*Thomas A. Kempis*

I have come to see that within my revelation of abject powerlessness is the very strength I have been seeking. It doesn't belong to me. I can only borrow on its promise, one day at a time.

I have known that alcohol has been a Power greater than me. How many times have I attempted to quit drinking? How many times have I sworn to stop the anguish? The real question for me in Step Two is whether this Power is capable of returning me to sanity. I have had my door open to the possibility of powers greater than myself in Step One. Now the acid test: is there one capable of returning me to sanity?

I transform this Second Step into a spiritual reality when I become comfortable with believing. Just as I am comfortable using my mind to help me cross a busy intersection, my belief in this Power can help me every time I pass a bar, or every time I get a little thirsty. The conscious or unconscious mind cannot help.

The mind as a rational instrument creates options. The mind allows me to dream of new transportation and communication systems. It helps make my work easier by inventing computers and nuclear energy. The mind does not understand that it is turned off after the first drink. Alcohol takes over the mind. Alcohol for the alcoholic is bigger than the mind. Nobody ever thought their way into sobriety. To do justice to my overworked mind, I must let it rest. The mind is not a player in developing a belief. The mind can be the enemy.

*Trust that man in nothing who has not a conscience in everything.*
*Laurence Sterne*

# STEP THREE

Made a decision to turn our will and our lives over to the care of God *as we understood Him.*

## Evening Prayers and Reflections for Trust

## Morning Promises and Reflections of Faith

## Evening Prayer 3:1

*Canst thou by searching find out God?*
*Bible*

**The moment has come to fall before Thee.** I have had my will broken, crushed into infinitesimal pieces. My life is shattered, hammered down by acts of my own making. I present to Thee this life and this will. I surrender myself to Thee. Accept this surrender moment by moment. Deal lightly with me, I beg Thee. There seems to be nothing left in me. If I move, I will know it is Thee moving in me. Now is the time. Amen.

*We should find God in what we do know, not in what we don't; not in outstanding problems, but in those we have already solved.*
*Dietrich Bonhoeffer*

## Evening Reflection 3:1

*God is the perfect poet, who in his person acts his own creations.*
*Robert Browning*

The prayer of the Third Step is one of trust. As I make the decision to turn my will and life over to the care of God, I accomplish what is a miracle to me. I am trusting that something I cannot control will take charge over all my affairs. In this Third Step, I am returning to the faith of a child.

This Step is not about understanding a complicated theological concept. I am not embracing a set of dogma and traditions that seem foreign and mysterious to me. My first instinct is to be insulted that any thinking, rational, 20th century person could subscribe to such a belief. I scream, "Don't you understand? Things are so much more complicated than that! If I were to just turn my will and my life over to something I cannot understand, then whole sections of my universe would fall down. How can I trust in anything so simple?"

*If I ascend up into heaven, thou [God] are there: if I make my bed in hell, behold, thou art there.*
*Bible*

## Evening Prayer 3:2

*God is seen God in the star, in the stone, in the flesh, in the soul and the clod.*
*Robert Browning*

**O Nameless One**, I have seen the possibility of believing in something that does not seek to destroy me. I am tired of carrying on my back the tragedy of my life. The promise of sanity, of reality and truth no longer scares me. I have learned to watch others, and I want what they have. I recognize I must take the most important step of my life, make the most important decision I will ever be called on to make. I have not been able to trust myself with life nor with death. I know I have not been a good master to myself. I ask you, oh Father, to forever free me from my bondage to myself. I want only to trust in you. Weariness with serving my own ends has put me on my knees. As I lay prostrate before Thee, I make this prayer. Amen.

*He who, from zone to zone, guides through the boundless sky thy certain flight, in the long way that I must tread alone, will lead my steps aright.*
*William Cullen Bryant*

## Evening Reflection 3:2

*Though God's attributes are equal yet his mercy is more attractive and pleasing in our eyes than his justice.*
*Cervantes*

Trust is knowing with God you are at home. Every time I attempted this step as a drunk, I came at it from a position of having power. I thought with power came knowledge, understanding, and control. My search was for something tangible and perceptibly real. I made the mistaken assumption that the search was for an individual or an institution to whom I could turn over my life. I found the constraints of organized religion too tight. I needed a more free flowing form. I adopted at different times all shapes and colors of New Age expressions.

All in all, I found institutions of all kinds to be monolithic and personally unsettling. I seemed always to gravitate to an individual. I found a guru, a human being that seemed to be a transmitter from God. As Joe had a better connection with God than I did, I thought I would be safe in absolute obedience to his will. This of course made my life easier as I could simply plug into Joe's will to find my own. I saw in Joe what belonged to God. I imitated Joe's ways. I copied his humanity and saw in that humanity the actions of the supernatural. I could not have been more wrong. The actions of another human being are simply the actions of a human being. It was Joe's business to live his own life. I had no business asking Joe to live mine.

*Theist and Atheist: The fight between them is as to whether God shall be called God or shall have some other name.*
*Samuel Butler*

## Evening Prayer 3:3

*Only this I know, that one celestial father gives to all.*
*Milton*

**O God** - Was it you I saw that September evening? I should have perished that night. Why did I not die? My fear was in living, not dying. When I was mugged and beaten and tossed over that bridge to die, why was the natural course of history rewritten? Why does it take so much to break my will? Why did I wander so long, so alone, so miserable? I question everything, and my mind tricks me often. It plays with my heart. It makes gods out of people. Oh, let me unconditionally love and serve you. I shall wonder now only what You would have for me. It was my own will that died underneath that bridge. Amen.

*If any man obeys the gods, they listen to him also.*
*Homer*

## Evening Reflection 3:3

*Everyone, whether he is self-denying or self-indulgent, is seeking after the Beloved. Every place may be the shrine of love, whether it be mosque or synagogue.*
*Hafiz*

Step Three allows me to once and forever distinguish between God and man. I cannot turn my will and my life over to a man or a woman. What on earth would one of my own kind do with my life? Every human being that has ever lived has had his or her hands full living their own life. Men and women who attempt to take on the lives of other people are operating with the mistaken idea they are God. When I pretend to be that which I am not, I am always hog tied by the lie.

My own God-man did the most mortal thing of all; he died. All I had left was the memory of his will for me, and that was not enough. The more the memory faded, the more confusing everything became. I had no trust in God, and therefore no trust in anyone or anything. The real power emerged -- John Barleycorn. All the power-driven schemes and the self-inflated victory stories were only illustrations of the supremacy of alcohol's illusions.

*God is day and night, winter and summer, war and peace, satiety and want.*
*Heraclitus*

## Evening Prayer 3:4

*As he that fears God fears nothing else, so, he that sees God sees every thing else.*
*John Donne*

**O God**, this name I address you by is filled with old images of a brash and brutal judge. The faith of my ancestors seems shut off to me. I have felt so abandoned by the historical church that I cannot see a way back. My eyes have been opened to a different kind of Higher Power. This Power invites me to trust, to believe, to have faith, to know that I am loved, I am accepted, I am forgiven, that the future is open. I feel enveloped by its love and filled with a wonderful spirit of promise. Maybe later, oh God, I will be able to connect the faith of the ages with my current decision to take Step Three. I know what I have done in Step Three works. It is the most important decision I have ever made. Amen.

*A believer, a mind whose faith is consciousness, is never disturbed because other persons do not yet see the fact which he sees.*
*Emerson*

## Evening Reflection 3:4

*If your faith is opposed to experience, to human learning and investigation, it is not worth the breath used in giving it expression.*
*Edgar Watson Howe*

I have only a mustard seed of faith. I bring that seed to the garden with the promise that it will grow. I see things more clearly now. My perspective on life is changing. I feel my anxiety quieting down. I no longer value my own works as more important than anyone else's. I am content now to be less than everything and more than nothing. You pick the spot for me, and I'll stand there. You pick the position for me, and I'll play it. I am Yours to do with as you will. Thank You for guiding me.

The promise of faith is like no other promise. Faithfulness will be like no other struggle. I can forever count on the fact that God will rule the world. I can forever count on the fact that I have a role, a most integral role, in that world, revealed to me on a day-to-day basis.

The will of God for me becomes discernible only as I near my appointed moment. I try to see into the future and find myself hopelessly lost in all the options available to me. Time has a fascinating way of limiting those options. Try as an ant will to have a perspective other than that of an ant, the efforts are all for naught. The ant can only see what an ant can see. If an ant could see world wide vegetable gardens and all the poor human beings fed, would this give the ant any more joy?

If I could see all there was about the future, about the universe, about the workings of God's will, would it make me more serene, happy, or human? How much would I understand; how much could I handle? The dark force we fight is the desire to be God, like Adam and Eve who were tempted to eat from the tree of knowledge of Good and Evil. It was clear from the beginnings of human history that I cannot become God. Absolute knowledge of Good and Evil is only in God's realm, not mine. My banishment from peace and serenity during my drinking days felt as cruel, as cold, as harsh as the banishment of Adam and Eve from the Garden of Paradise.

*The care of God for us is a great thing, if man believe it at heart: it plucks the burden of sorrow from him.*
*Euripides*

## Morning Promise 3:1

*You can do very little with faith, but you can do nothing without it.*
*Samuel Butler*

Surprise! Surprise! Surprise! There are truly seasons to the year. Spring does follow winter. There is light after darkness. Rainbows do show themselves after a summer rain. Barren trees do sprout buds and renew their lives each year. The Power that can snatch life away is the same Power that infuses new life. I am not dead. More importantly, I do not wish to be dead. If I have faith, the judgment on my life is also my mercy. The promise of faith is a gift, not an act of will but rather a discovery of a deep intense love.

*A faith that sets bounds to itself, that will believe so much and no more, that will trust thus far and no further, is none.*
*Julius Charles Hare & Augustus William Hare*

## Morning Reflection 3:1

*Faith is to believe what you do not yet see; the reward for this faith is to see what you believe.*
*St. Augustine*

Faith is a promise that begins as an acorn and grows into an oak tree. Have you ever watched an ant? The little creature is filled with energy, industriousness and strength. Sometimes it will be hauling a twig six times its own size.

You begin to play with the ant. You have it crawl up your hand. You move it from one hand to the other. You walk over to the hood of your car and watch it busily carry its load up your windshield. You place the ant on your sleeve and up it goes.

Now suppose you could hear the protestations of this ant. "Look Sir," he says, "I have things to do. I am part of this big colony, and we are building things in that colony that will change the course of our ant history. I would appreciate it if you would quit screwing around with me and let me get back to my business."

You ignore the ant's self-importance. The ant gets riled and begins to kick you with his little foot. He kicks so hard he falls over. He says, "So there! If you don't lay off, I'll kick you some more." The ant is determined to have his way. You say, "Well, I don't understand how this colony of yours is so important, but if you insist on living with this belief, I'll let you go." The ant immediately goes back to hauling his twig and building his little ant colony near a hedge row on your neighbor's property.

After a few days, the ant and his mates have built a little ant hill. It seems all their efforts have finally paid off. Then your neighbor comes out one morning to do some weeding, preparing his hedge row for the fall. In one giant swipe he tears down the ant hill, unwittingly burying it in mounds of dirt. No more ant colony; this thing that was going to change the course of ant history is suddenly finished.

How many times have my own plans been smashed to pieces? Faith is knowing there is a plan, one that often begins at the moment my own plans are destroyed.

*To believe only possibilities is not faith, but mere philosophy.*
*Sir Thomas Browne*

## Morning Promise 3:2

*He's a Blockhead who wants a proof of what he can't Perceive, and he's a Fool who tries to make such a Blockhead believe.*
*William Blake*

An old woman known for wisdom admonished me often on the subject of faith. She would say, "You can have faith in all manner of things as long as you do not place that faith in yourself. You can believe in all manner of things as long as you resist the temptation to believe in yourself. Have faith only in that which brought you here and remain loyal only to that which will lead you out." The woman would offer me no advice on any special subject. She would ignore me when I asked her about my problems with relationships, with business, with the government. She would only smile when I reported I was finally getting control over my life. When I was dragged low with pain she would hold me like a baby, but on the issue of faith she would vary not one inch. Have faith only in God and have only one God.

*Console thyself, thou wouldst not seek Me, if thou hadst not found Me.*
*Pascal*

## Morning Reflection 3:2

*Faith is the substance of things hoped for, the evidence of things not seen.*
*Bible*

The neighbor has no idea that he is responsible for the ant's tragedy. His act took all of 30 seconds, and he is now back in his house eating a cookie. The insult to the ant is great. He carries himself to the foot of the neighbor's door and calls out to him.

"You bastard! You ruined something that took me a lifetime to build. If you dare come out here, I'll kick your ass so hard you won't be able to remember your name. How could you do this to me and my friends? Have you no feelings? Didn't you realize what we were doing? Our whole colony was counting on this thing we were building and you ruined it all."

The neighbor comes out after finishing his cookie and walks directly into the ant's path. The ant holds his ground. The neighbor steps on the ant; and Mr. Ant is gone, finished. The other ants see this and run for cover.

The neighbor decides that he has a better idea for the area around his hedge row. He creates a vegetable garden and gets a beautiful crop of vegetables.

All the neighbors take note of this innovative use of space. The old timers remember the war years when everyone was encouraged to have victory gardens. Soon everybody around is transforming their yard into a garden. It becomes a most noteworthy affair. People begin to drive through the neighborhood and marvel at the plentiful vegetables the small gardens are producing. Children of all sizes and shapes beg their parents to let them start such projects in their own yards.

After awhile the newspaper and television people pick up on this phenomenon. People all over the city become self-sufficient in vegetables. Hundreds of yards are transformed into great and glorious gardens. Some of the gardeners plan to send their crops to places experiencing famine.

Faith is knowing I don't have to know the outcome. Faith is realizing I am part of the plan. Faith is knowing that my role in the plan is crucial and that it is not the only role. The admonition in Step Three is to Let Go and Let God.

*The relation of faith between subject and object is unique in every case. Hundreds may believe, but each has to believe by himself.*
*W.H. Auden*

## Morning Promise 3:3

*If every gnat that flies were an archangel, all that could but tell me is that there is a God; and the poorest worm that creeps tells me that.*
*John Donne*

How is it that absolutely every time I elect to trust in this Higher Power of mine, things seem to work out? Why is it that every time I am called on to turn my will over to my Higher Power, I fight it with every fiber in my being? My rational mind fights with spiritual discipline at every point. The promise of faith is unfailing in its ability to deliver what is best for me. Whether in deciding about a job, entering a relationship, raising children, or changing a habit pattern, Step Three is always our anchor. Faith is not my newest manifestation of will power. It is life's oldest testament to the Power that really runs the universe. When I embrace this promise, I connect myself to the single greatest all-determining reality there has ever been or will ever be. Amen.

*No one has the capacity to judge God. We are drops in that limitless ocean of mercy.*
*Mohandas K. Gandhi*

## Morning Reflection 3:3

*The way of God is complex, he is hard for us to predict. He moves the pieces and they come somehow into a kind of order.*
*Euripides*

If Mr. Ant could have understood that there was a Power greater than he and that Power had great things in store for him and his colony, then Mr. Ant could have shared in the event that was going to change not only ant history, but human history. But Mr. Ant could not get outside his own universe to see that he was just a part of a bigger picture. When the bigger picture impinged on his world, all he could do was shake his fist and martyr himself for something small and insignificant.

My decision in Step Three is to trust that such a picture exists, that the picture has a role for me. I am not the whole picture, but my role is important and significant. All my attempts at making myself the whole picture, making my anthill the end product of creation, got me nowhere and nothing but misery. My decision to trust in God and turn my will and my life over to Him will claim for me a place in His victory of all creation.

*The only money of God is God. He pays never with any thing less, or any thing else.*
*Emerson*

## Morning Promise 3:4

*Faith is a living and unshakeable confidence, a belief in the grace of God so assured that a man would die a thousand deaths for its sake.*
*Martin Luther*

I remember an instance that seems to describe the promise of the Third Step. I was anguishing over a divorce. I was young and very insecure. She did not like me, let alone love me. My heart was broken; my self-image was the lowest. I read everything I could find on marriage, divorce, relationships, positive self-image. Nothing made me feel better. I could understand intellectually what the words meant, yet they did not penetrate to the core of my being. I knew when I got married that I had made a mistake. The morning after our first night together as husband and wife I remember going out for coffee for the two of us. As I waited for service my heart sank to my feet. I just knew that this thing that I had done the day before was wrong. Yet I could not face the consequences of a bad choice. It would be four years of trial, torment and despair before I would face up to the consequences of that single act. Step Three is not about miraculous changed consequences. God does not make our decisions. When we trust God we learn we can live with our consequences. Moreover we need not be forever chained to bad choices. We are free to make the right decision for our lives.

*Faith, like a jackal, feeds among the tombs, and even from these dead doubts she gathers her most vital hope.*
*Herman Melville*

## Morning Reflection 3:4

*Faith is not a formula which is agreed to if the weight of evidence favors it.*
*Walter Lippmann*

The victory that awaits me in the promise of the Third Step is that once and for all I can count on something which will never betray me. I will no longer have to chain myself to illusions about life. I let mortal men be mortal men, for I have allowed God to be God. I am faithful to my decision to let my will and my life be determined by my Higher Power. What this does is put me in touch with the larger picture.

Just like the ant who was only aware of his own ant colony, I could only see my ant hill. Ants with Higher Powers become connected to the larger plan. Even when they don't understand why their ant hill is being plowed under, they have faith that God has a larger plan in mind. I embrace God, placing my trust in this enigmatic power that I cannot comprehend. I inherit a victory and a success that is infinitely beyond my ability to either appreciate or replicate. Mr. Ant was actually part of a plan to feed the world, yet he only saw himself building the best ant hill on the block.

Faith is not the answer to the prayer. Faith is the inevitable result of the person who trusts God absolutely.

*Not truth, but Faith, it is, that keeps the world alive.*
*Edna St. Vincent Millay*

# STEP FOUR

Made a searching and fearless moral inventory of ourselves.

## Evening Prayers and Reflections for Honesty

## Morning Promises and Reflections of Illumination

## Evening Prayer 4:1

*Who cannot open an honest mind, no friend will he be of mine.*
*Euripides*

**Now that I am armed with my decision,** I dare to name this Power that loves me more than I love myself. I call You God, Abba, Father. I ask for Your mercy, Your tender understanding. You know I have lived in the shadowy recesses of life. I have been gripped by fear since the day I was born. I have been blind to the fact that reality would not harm me. I have consistently run from my life. I have so much to share with You. I ask for moments of fearless courage as I write my inventory. I can't yet imagine myself living the entire day without fear. But please, Oh God, provide me with enough courage to tell my story to You. Amen.

*Honesty's praised, then left to freeze.*
*Juvenal*

## Evening Reflection 4:1

*To state the facts frankly is not to despair for the future nor indict the past.*
*John F. Kennedy*

Honesty has been for me a most illusive characteristic. When I live in a fog of deceit, honesty becomes a meaningless concept. Insane behavior breeds its own kind of twisted honesty. At best I make periodic vain attempts at explaining or justifying my behavior. I shade experiences with my own blend of half truths and self-serving rationalizations. I fear the truth like the Wicked Witch of the East feared water. I believe if the truth were known I would disappear. The operative word in this struggle to live in a make believe world is fear. Fear rules supreme. All communications and actions stand first in judgment with my fear quotient. I would elevate myself to levels of self-importance and convince myself that others cared about my shading of the truth.

There is no long-term recovery without honesty. All other virtues begin to make sense after honesty is fully grasped. Without honesty I cannot see where I am. If I am ever to move beyond this point, I need to see where I am.

There has not been a soul who walked the earth who has not had to clean the slate. It seems impossible to do the will of God on a daily basis. There is always need for personal housecleaning. My aunt could never understand the business of clearing up the past. Neither family persuasion nor an eight week treatment center could open her to the possibility of doing an inventory of her life. She came out of a treatment program with 70 years of baggage she refused to let go -- tons of guilt, heaps of regrets, scores of amends that she had no power to make without a thorough housecleaning. Four months after she left the treatment center, she had a stroke. It locked her in a twilight zone of reality. She lost virtually all short-term memory. All that was left was long-term memory, filled with regret, sadness, and fear. She will never get better. She will remain as she is until death.

I now realize what it would be like to live in that kind of purgatory. I have potential as a human being, but I have allowed my self-esteem to drop too low to see any real character. My aunt must make her peace with the world some other way. I see from the illumination in Step Four that a thorough and honest inventory is a much easier route.

*I have no idea what the mind of a lowlife scoundrel is like, but I know what the mind of an honest man is like: it is terrifying.*
*Abel Hermant*

## Evening Prayer 4:2

*The confession of one man humbles all.*
*Antonio Porchia*

**O Keeper Of The Gate**, as I stand before You I am called to believe Judgment Day has arrived. I was brought into life alone. I stand before You alone, with no crutches. I am not here with a wife, a relationship, a bottle, pill or drug, a degree, a job, my looks, my personality, my car, my future deals, my friends, my therapist, my books, my opinions, my good intentions, my outrage, my excuses, my confessor, priest or rabbi. I am here alone and naked. I present to You the lessons of my work. My inventory is complete. I await Your forgiveness. Amen.

*Confession of our faults is the next thing to innocence.*
*Publilius Syrus*

## Evening Reflection 4:2

*Though the mills of God grind slowly, yet they grind exceeding small; though with patience He stands waiting, with exactness grinds He all.*
*Friedrich Von Logau*

Step Four is telling the truth about my life. It is not explaining, justifying or apologizing for my actions. Step Four is seeing how things have actually been. The spiritual cloak of honesty envelops me in the protection afforded me in the Third Step. I became one step removed from myself. I have turned over to God my will and my life.

That decision tells me that anything and everything that happens hereafter is in God's hands. This certainly includes my past life. God never deserted me; it is I who deserted God. As I work on my inventory detail by detail, year by year, instance by instance, uncovering everything, I am constantly turning more to God. It almost feels like my past life is fertilizer, fueling my new life. I will tell it all, be rigorously thorough.

I become faint in the midst of this inventory writing, particularly when I begin to probe the darker corners of my history. I have learned in my earlier steps the spiritual categories of fortitude. I have seen how others maintain a steadfast faith one day at a time. It is toward faith I move as the result of my inventory.

My prayer for honesty is secure in the knowledge that nothing of any consequence can befall me when I tell the truth. Honesty directly connects me to my Higher Power. Honesty keeps me ever mindful of my relationship with God. Now is the time to stop the misery.

*It is not the criminal things which are hardest to confess, but the ridiculous and shameful.*
*Rousseau*

## Evening Prayer 4:3

*I hope I shall always possess firmness and virtue enough to maintain what I consider the most enviable of all titles, the character of an "Honest Man."*
*George Washington*

**O Lord Of My Dreams**, I find myself waking up, like Rip Van Winkle, from a twenty-year sleep. I look around and see a strange new world. I do not understand a world that is not treacherous. I feel I have lived my whole life perched precariously on a mile-high ledge, unable to let go because I will fall into the abyss. Now that I have my eyes open, I see there is this staircase down from the ledge. All I have to do is climb. Oh God, how could this be? How could I be set free from my hellish existence? The voice I hear says, "Come forth." I shall come... now. Amen.

*No legacy is so rich as honesty.*
*Shakespeare*

## Evening Reflection 4:3

*Honesty is for the most part less profitable than dishonesty.*
*Plato*

The first thing to know as I pray for honesty is there really is no downside to telling truth. Truth brings me sanity and allows me to live in the real world. Honesty keeps me standing in the midst of truth.

I am confronted with decisions on how I shall handle the truth. Truth has no degrees. I am either honest, or I am not. Shades are man-made.

A sheep wanders away from its flock, taking a little nibble here, a little nibble there. It soon loses touch with the other sheep. It is lost.

So it is with lying. I tell a little lie here, I shade the truth there, and soon I lose touch with reality. I no longer see where I was, I am terribly unfamiliar with where I am, and I have no idea where I am going.

I fervently pray for a guardian angel to show me how to get back to my flock. It never happens that way. The tapestry of deceit does not lend itself to being unwoven all at once. I find my way back by searching and fearless nibbles, uncovering the truth one step at a time.

*Honesty is a good thing but it is not profitable to its possessor unless it is kept under control. If you are not honest at all everybody hates you and if you are absolutely honest you get martyred.*
*Don Marquis*

## Evening Prayer 4:4

*And if any mischief follow, then thou shalt give life for life, eye for eye, tooth for tooth, hand for hand, foot for foot, burning for burning, wound for wound, stripe for stripe.*
*Bible*

**O Father**, my confession to You is now complete. I have revealed all I am -- or at least all I can remember about myself. I place this before You with humility. I beg You to love me. I am Yours. I am turning myself over to You. I confess I only remember You as a vengeful Spirit. I have spent most of my life mortally afraid of You. Now I trust what others say when they speak of an Almighty God who loves completely, intimately and with boundless forgiveness. Please be that for me. I am raw and hurting and want only to be reconciled to You who love me. Amen.

*There's no need to hang about waiting for the Last Judgment - it takes place every day.*
*Albert Camus*

## Evening Reflection 4:4

*God gives each his due at the time allotted.*
*Euripides*

The prayer for honesty is a profoundly challenging one for me. I must rely on my Third Step to be ready for Step Four. If I have embraced my Higher Power, this should make me ready to get on with living.

I feel as if I am perched atop a high platform. Below me is a pool of water eight inches deep. I can barely see the water from where I stand. All I have to do is follow instructions and jump.

I am filled with doubt. I think, "Don't people realize that I can't jump from this height into a pool of water only eight inches deep?" The more I think about it, the more far-fetched the whole idea becomes. One excuse after another pours into my mind. Finally my mind says, "Get off this platform!"

As I turn, I see a harness I can wear. It will protect me from hurting myself. All I have to do is attach the harness to myself and jump. But I am used to turning down any and all offers of help. I have been so self-willed throughout my life that the thought of obtaining help seems ludicrous. If I can't do it all by myself, I won't do it at all. What I am really saying is if my fear tells me I can do something, then I can do it. My fear level guides my actions.

The only thing that was ever able to control my fear was liquor. Not only did it deaden my fear, it deadened every other human instinct I had. So on top of this platform I realize that my fear is instructing me to get off. My mind reminds me that if I don't do something about the fear, it will not instruct my body to jump. The old solution to this dilemma would be to drink.

The fact is, with alcohol in my system I could leap in the wrong direction. The chief judge of my actions has always been fear. If I can remove fear, then reflexes be damned - I'll go for it. In that world I am yet one more casualty.

My Fourth Step prayer for honesty allows me to put on the harness and turn my fear over to it. I am not asked to give up my body to quell my fear. I am merely asked to trust a Power greater than myself to see me through this dilemma. The harness has worked for countless years. It has never failed. It will never fail. God is an eternal harness.

*The gods visit the sins of the fathers upon the children.*
*Euripides*

## Morning Promise 4:1

*A man who permits his honor to be taken, permits his life to be taken.*
*Pietro Aretino*

Discovering my own life is unmistakably good. I am more loving and deserving of love. When I turn a bright light on all corners of my past and present, so much goodness is revealed. The things I used to beat myself up with don't exist anymore. I am forgiven. All that is good awaits me when I turn my back on fear. The little scared people inside me are allowed to grow.

*He that is faithful in that which is least is faithful also in much; and he that is unjust in the least is unjust also in much.*
*Bible*

## Morning Reflection 4:1

*Honor is like a steep island without a shore: one cannot return once one is outside.*
*Nicolas Boileau*

The promise that breaks through in the dark night as I write my inventory is illumination. The cry, "I can see! I can see!" pours forth from my heart. For what may be the first time, I can see my life for what it was, the patterns, the contours of my personality.

Step Four inventory allows no halfhearted explanations of my life experiences. Cold hard truth is there, well documented and plain to see. The facts do not bear out the guilt I have heaped upon myself. Quite the contrary. I see a very young person who throughout life seemed to be repeating hurtful behavior time after time. The tragedy was I was helpless to stop this self-abuse.

Illumination! When I was a boy my dad would leave every Monday morning and be gone for a week. He would return on Friday, after he stopped off at a friend's home for a few drinks. When he came home, there was always a great deal of charm, humor and special surprises for his five demanding little children. What little I saw of Dad I liked. When Dad stayed around for any length of time, though, he would become impatient with us, and inevitably lost his temper. His anger was fierce. I would feel utterly and completely rejected. I remember as many goodbyes as hellos, as many hits as hugs.

One day, when I was thirteen, the priest came to our house to see us. This had never happened before. He gathered the children downstairs while a friend of Mother's spoke with her in her bedroom.

The priest told us that Dad had passed away the night before. My mind raced to locate a meaning for the words, "passed away." I refused to land on the meaning of "died." I leaped up and screamed that there must be something I could do. He said NO! Categorically, finally and firmly. Your Dad is dead.

I rocked back in my chair, unable to hear. I was learning about pain for the first time in my life. Death was too final; anything was better. My father couldn't be dead.

I sat in my chair and built an iron wall around my feelings, with a sentry at the gate. Death would never enter my heart again.

*Would that the simple maxim, that honesty is the best policy, might be laid to heart; that a sense of the true aim of life might elevate the tone of politics and trade till public and private honor become identical.*
*Margaret Fuller*

## Morning Promise 4:2

*The just man, O Xerxes, walks humbly in the presence of his God, but walks fearlessly.*
*Walter Savage Landor*

My younger brother played the role of Biff Loman in the Arthur Miller play, "Death of a Salesman." What a role for him to play. What a play for my family to see. The stark reality of unmasking the truth in the Loman family was upsetting to me. How Biff Loman reminded me of me! My Third Step decision empowers me to embrace the truth about life. "Death of a Salesman" is about one family's inability to come to terms with failure. Is not failure our inability to come to terms with reality? Reality is not failure; it is being loved by God.

*Integrity without knowledge is weak and useless, and knowledge without integrity is dangerous and dreadful.*
*Samuel Johnson*

## Morning Reflection 4:2

*To be individually righteous is the first of all duties, come what may to one's self, to one's country, to society, and to civilization itself.*
*Joseph Wood Krutch*

When my father died, I ran to my mother so I could take care of her, so I would not have to focus on my own feelings. Mother was already attending to herself, behind a closed door. I went downstairs to seek another form of escape--a book. I learned I could get lost in other people's lives at times of great personal sorrow. I was one step removed from sorrow when it belonged to someone else.

During the ensuing days, I watched the proceedings with detachment. My emotional wall held back the torrent of sadness waiting to pour in. Time and again, male friends promised they would be a Dad to me and my brothers and sisters, or told me, "You will have to be the man of the house now."

I hated the phony sentiment about a man many of these people barely knew nor liked. I just wanted the funeral and wake to be over. Life was never the same after that. I was never the same. I had learned to shut down. It would become my life's pattern.

The promise of illumination was brilliant and strong for me after my Fourth Step. As I relive my life, I see the cement I poured over my Dad's death, the iron wall I built, the sentry who faithfully guarded passage to my emotions for more than 20 years.

Armed with trust and faith from Step Three, I met this sentry and thanked him for his time. I explained I had a new guard, God, Who would now protect me. I said I appreciated his faithful service over the years, but it was time for him to leave. I gave him a hug and sent him on his way.

Now I was ready to go to work. I had to break down the wall. If I was to be searching and fearless, I had to expose this pivotal event to the light of day. So much would be illuminated in my life if I could only examine the circumstances surrounding my Father's death.

*A man of honor should never forget what he is because he sees what others are.*
*Balthasar Gracian*

## Morning Promise 4:3

*This above all: to thine own self be true, and it must follow, as the night the day, thou canst not then be false to any man.*
*Shakespeare*

Every time I think of Martin Luther King's "I have a dream" speech, I am reminded what it is to live with one foot in the grave. When we can accept death, we can talk of a world with illuminating vitality. When we can accept our past, we can anticipate the future. The dream Martin spoke of was magnificent; it described a world where God ruled. The dreams I used to dream where I ruled were all nightmares. Those were the dreams that caused me to wake in a cold sweat. It is dreaming about God's dream that I now choose. God's promise for me is the only promise for me. Let me become a child and awaken to the promise of walking with other children who belong to God. I, too, have a dream...

*The truth is, hardly any of us have ethical energy enough for more than one really inflexible point of honor.*
*George Bernard Shaw*

## Morning Reflection 4:3

*We acknowledge our faults in order to repair by our sincerity the damage they have done us in the eyes of others.*
*La Rochefoucauld*

I locked myself in a hotel room when I decided to write my inventory. My list was long and searching. I found so many resentments, so much anger, fear and sadness. The deeper I dug, the more I saw.

First, the death of my father cut off the possibility of resolving my issues with him as a dad. At 13, I had a powerful resentment for him. His anger and beatings were a source of much frustration for me. How could he die without first clearing things up with me? The authority he assumed over my life and the manner in which he exercised that authority caused me deep resentment.

What was illuminating in Step Four was how I took my resentment for my Dad's authority into all other places in life in which I experienced authority. I resented everything from hall monitors in schools to traffic lights. Whether it was the draft board, an employer, the vice principal or religion, I was at war with authority.

I found I hated the men and women who promised to be there after my dad died. They were basically good people, trying to say the things that would comfort me. I saw them as chameleons and phonies. I rejected them and anyone who tried to help me. I was determined to be self-sufficient.

My inventory showed me how my self-sufficiency cut me off from many opportunities to interact with people. Whenever anyone got too close, I would freeze them out. Intimacy creates the risk of being hurt.

Mother never recovered from Dad's death. She dealt with her loneliness with alcohol. What a portent this was for me. As she prepared for her first drink of the day, she was always a bundle of nervous confusion. After her first drink, she was awash in boozy sentiment. Either way, she was lost to us. Emotionally, she died with my dad.

Living with my mother became an emotional roller coaster. She could be trusted to impose guilt and shame upon us all. Nothing was ever quite right. We came to assume all things would have a tragic ending.

My Irish friends call this condition the Celtic Twilight. Darkness was never far off. This message emanated from Mother, and I came to equate the message with the messenger. Mother became women in general. Women became the bearers of bad news.

The Fourth Step illuminated my crippled environment. My world view was created during that time. My relationships with women were a part of that distorted view.

*How happy is he born and taught, that serveth not another's will; whose armour is his honest thought, and simple truth his utmost skill.*
*Sir Henry Wotton*

## Morning Promise 4:4

*A moment's insight is sometimes worth a life's experience.*
*Oliver Wendell Holmes, Sr.*

I await the illuminating experience of resurrection. Writing my inventory has exhausted me. I have resolutely held to the truth about every episode of my life. I await the moment of rebirth. I feel as Jesus must have when he spoke the words, "It is finished." I am laying down my burdens and hold tightly to the promise that the rock will be rolled back.

*To understand is to forgive, even oneself.*
*Alexander Chase*

## Morning Reflection 4:4

*Let my heart be wise. It is the gods' best gift.*
*Euripides*

Perhaps the most poignant illumination in the inventory came in my relationship with God. Catholicism formed my religious beliefs. The God of my beliefs was a harsh judge of those who strayed from the Church. Errant actions were treated with terrifying pain.

I knew my dad was not the most devout of Catholics. I overheard too many fights with Mother, and was the object of his wrath on too many occasions, to think otherwise. I wondered at his death if my dad had done anything to square himself with God. I had my doubts. Where was Dad spending eternity?

My father and I fought frequently in the days before he died. Perhaps I had indirectly caused his death? Could I be responsible for my Father's eternal damnation? I really didn't believe such a thing, but maybe ...

It seemed so simple taking an inventory, honestly looking at the events of my life. Yet prior to Step Three, nothing gripped me with more fear. After completing my inventory, the fear subsided. The patterns were illuminated. I confronted the fact that without a Higher Power, there was very little truth I could swallow. Whatever I had for a Higher Power as a child, it was not something I could rely on as an adult to help me face the truth.

The Fourth Step revealed an ordinary person making an extraordinary ordeal out of realities most people have to deal with on a daily basis. The crosses that I bore were mostly those of my own creation. The truth I came to see was that fear controlled my every move.

Alcohol was a release from fear. Alcohol was a replacement for a Higher Power. The inventory precisely described the result of a life lived without benefit of a Higher Power. All the futile attempts at taking control over my own life were fully illuminated. The patterns were revealed, the truth exposed, poised to set me free.

*All persons are puzzles until at last we find in some word or act the key to the man, to the woman; straightway all their past words and actions lie in light before us.*
*Emerson*

# STEP FIVE

Admitted to God, to ourselves, and to another human being the exact nature of our wrongs.

## Evening Prayers and Reflections for Courage

## Morning Promises and Reflections of Forgiveness

## Evening Prayer 5:1

*The ineffable joy of forgiving and being forgiven forms an ecstasy that might well arouse the envy of the gods.*
*Elbert Hubbard*

**O That Which Listens Patiently To My Every Cry,** I pray for the courage to reveal myself and all that I have so nearly thrown away. I have carefully selected the person with whom I will share the details of this Fourth Step. I know that the love that I feel is divine and is not owned by anyone, nor withdrawn for any reason. It is only I who can deny myself this love by turning my back on You. I pray for the courage to foursquarely face this other person and speak the words of the Fourth Step. I so desire to be finished with all that has hurt me. Amen.

*We pardon as long as we love.*
*La Rochefoucauld*

## Evening Reflection 5:1

*Nothing comes from nothing.*
*Lucretius*

There can be no hesitating about my Fifth Step. The courage to be honest surges into me once I utter my Third Step prayer. I remember that, with my Third Step, I have forever placed myself in the proper relationship with God.

Courage becomes something sensitive and healing to me. It is safe for me to be vulnerable. I am strong when I feel my weaknesses. My victory has already been won. Hope is the greatest power known to man. Courage is a gift from God. It has nothing to do with ego. Courage allows us to stand as a human being.

The first time I expose myself in my Fifth Step, one on one, I manifest courage. I am guaranteed that in all subsequent encounters with another human, courage will be with me. The truth is no longer to be feared.

I may experience exhilaration at the end of my Fifth Step, a surge of lightness from my encounter with honesty. I will look back on this Step and wonder just how it was it came to pass. Who was that person who was so explicitly and honestly telling the truth about his life? Could it have been me?

Not only was it me, but a me that I had never seen before, one who manifested bold courage. This was perhaps the first time in my whole life I was completely honest with another human being. I have courageously set my compass in a direction that points to peace and serenity.

*Our least deed, like the young of the land crab, wends its way to the sea of cause and effect as soon as born, and makes a drop there to eternity.*
*Thoreau*

## Evening Prayer 5:2

*Life only demands from you the strength you possess. One feat is possible - not to have run away.*
*Dag Hammarskjold*

**O Thou Wellspring Of Strength,** why is it so hard to hold the truth? Is truth hot? If I get too close will I be burned and ultimately destroyed? No. Truth is not hot; it is cold. It does not burn with heat; it burns like ice. It shimmers with cold hard clarity. It preserves as ice preserves. Courage to tell the truth protects our life. O God, cloak me with courage to be true, even if I shiver. Amen.

*People with courage and character always seem sinister to the rest.*
*Hermann Hesse*

## Evening Reflection 5:2

*This is courage in a man: to bear unflinchingly what heaven sends.*
*Euripides*

To my amazement, the Fifth Step did not release terror and humiliation in me. I wondered what had happened to the dragons I had so carefully hidden in the closet. I remembered the difficulty I had admitting to my alcoholism. I would go to such lengths to hide the quantity of my drinking. I used every kind of mouthwash available to disguise the smell of my breath. Somehow it would be all right as long as people didn't know. If

I could just keep the truth away, it would make my life better.

I was killing myself, and my primary concern was keeping the death a secret from my family and friends. Somehow they all would think less of me if I dared to die. My ego was a gigantic balloon waiting to be punctured. All of life was consumed with the fear that someone would come along and burst the balloon.

When I was lying in that Washington D.C. hospital, jaw wired shut, tubes coming out of all my orifices, bones broken, lung collapsed, all I could think about was getting a straw into a bottle of vodka. I was a very frightened young man.

Step Five presents an unquestionable opportunity to have courage that does not come from a bottle, courage born from the profound relationship between an individual soul and a Higher Power.

The frightening encounter with my father's death had resolved itself in my Fifth Step. I had lived my entire life after this event in suspenseful fear of anything like it ever happening again.

The shock of Dad's passing was so complete, all my emotions had been paralyzed. There had been no growth in many critical areas of my life. The Fifth Step started the thawing process, so that my locked-away emotions could break loose.

*Selfish persons are incapable of loving others, but they are not capable of loving themselves either.*
*Erich Fromm*

## Evening Prayer 5:3

*It is courage, courage, courage, that raises the blood of life to crimson splendor.*
*George Bernard Shaw*

**O Mother And Father Of All,** I ask that I become reconciled to my own mother and father. I am of their blood and spirit. I have worked at my relationship with them. I have felt our bond to be a crucifix upon which I died; at the same time, I have experienced it to be my one connection to life. Let me put down the scales on which I have judged these people. I ask that Thou provide me with the eyes to see my parents as a man and a woman loved by You as I am. Let me experience the bond of love that would bring our lives together. You are the source of all courage and the great reconciler of broken relationships. Amen.

*Courage is a kind of salvation.*
*Plato*

## Evening Reflection 5:3

***A liar will not be believed, even when he speaks the truth.***
***Aesop***

The meandering journey through the events of my past allowed me to take the white hot mantle of truth and melt through the iceberg that was formed around my feelings. Then, seeing them for what they were, all fear melted away.

Step Five proved that it takes more than time to heal wounds. Time must combine with honesty to heal a broken life. I placed on the stage of history all those broken relationships with people, who were forever subjected to my paralyzing unresponsiveness. I desperately yearned to give and feel what I know was richly deserved and deeply requested, but I had no way to unfreeze myself. Try as I would to find courage in myself, it never happened.

I am dealing with the most irrational of all human experiences: fear. Fear feeds on itself. Fear tells lies to protect itself. Fear distorts reality into its own form. Fear consumes and grows like wildfire. The courage to conquer fear is the beginning of spiritual revitalization.

We feel this courage in Step Five. Perhaps for the first time, we find that which has dominion over fear. Step Five reveals how fear distorts life. I saw that I had taken the sentiments of good people surrounding me after my Father's death, and made them caricatures. I had generalized my perceptions into wild opinions about the insensitivity of all mankind. I allowed this resentment to color all my subsequent relationships.

The fear of death became fear of dependency. Mother had never come to grips with death either. Her response to my Dad's passing was to cauterize her pain with alcohol. I resented her for this. I assumed since she was older, and my mother, she owed me her attention.

Her pain overwhelmed her. She had been a power greater than me throughout my life. Now it seemed that I was rejected by her. My mind magnified this desertion because my fear was so great. My mother's detachment became more significant to me than her problem with alcohol. I truly believed that there was something in the character of a woman that could not be trusted. I guarded myself from becoming too attached. I took only what I needed and left before the door slammed.

At 13, I made what seemed like a lifetime commitment to never trust people. I had never been required to give anything of myself. Dinner was always prepared, clothes were always pressed for school, the fuel bill was always paid. I felt it was my right to be safe and secure. A 13-year-old frozen in time and space can only embody a very small understanding of life. The discovery of alcohol insured that I would remain thirteen.

*One falsehood spoils a thousand truths.*
*Ashanti Proverb*

## Evening Prayer 5:4

*I would prefer even to fail with honor than win by cheating.*
*Sophocles*

**O Lord, Master Of All**, even the dark corners, courage seems to escape me at small moments. Why can't I get honest? Why do I sometimes inflate my successes? If I found $10,000 in cash on a street corner, would I turn the money over to the authorities? Would I exploit a situation with a vulnerable person? Would I report all my income to the I.R.S.? Since I have been honest about the past, will I be honest about the future? These are questions I bring before Thee. Perhaps courage must be something I draw on daily, or even moment to moment. I ask that You watch me, kick me gently as these occasions occur. Amen.

*He that lies on the ground cannot fall.*
*Yiddish Proverb*

## Evening Reflection 5:4

*No faith is our own that we have not arduously won.*
*Havelock Ellis*

There is something so magnificent about the truth, it is hard to understand why I fled from it. I am part of a species that regularly runs from lions, tigers, bears and the truth. The truth is so feared. My prayer for courage is that my long life of isolation be over.

The Fifth Step is not explaining, not rationalizing, but rather telling the truth. I specifically tell the truth to another human being and to God. I detail exactly what I uncovered in my Fourth Step. It takes courage to utter the words as they should be uttered. It seems so strange for me not to dress the truth up in a coat of many colors.

There is a saying that goes, "A person is only as sick as their secrets." The beginning of spiritual fulfillment is precisely at the place I disclose the truth about myself. Step Five allows me freedom from my secrets. Once I rid myself of this awful baggage, I can begin to fill my life with freshness and truth.

Secrets that are exposed to light dissolve into the air. The mere act of sharing with another person the exact details of my inventory allows me to declare that I no longer give these events a power over my life.

Hearing myself tell another person the details of my life clarifies who I am and what I am. My words spoken out loud in Step Five are my declaration of freedom from self. Speaking these words before God acknowledges that I am human, that I accept my humanity, and that I no longer wish to pretend I am in charge.

I found in my Fifth Step a reason for my isolation and loneliness. The selfishness that had been locked in, the world of relationships that had been locked out, drew me deeper into my own dark world. Step Five opened that world. Every new act of honesty brought a new source of courage.

The teenager I was can now become an adult. My generalized condemnations of life and God's creation can be set aside. Step Five opens the window to a less demanding and denigrating place. Each new challenge to tell the truth promises a new courageous opportunity to embrace the world as it is. With each new confirmation that the world is not a terrifying mistake, a wonderful bond with God unfolds.

When I am asked how I would describe my childhood, I no longer have to answer, "Long, my childhood was long." Step Five clears away the fog of deception. It throws open the doors of life and lets in the fresh winds of change. I feel as if I have been released from the shackles of the past. I am ready to get on with living, growing and loving.

Like the lion in the Wizard of Oz, I have found courage in my own back yard. I feel pure, forgiven and immensely thankful for being alive.

*Men fall from great fortune because of the same shortcomings that led to their rise.*
*La Bruyere*

## Morning Promise 5:1

*As contagion of sickness makes sickness, contagion of trust makes trust.*
*Marianne Moore*

Forgiveness is the promise that unlocks the door to a new life and allows me to live without resentments. My Fourth Step is strewn with the wreckage of a life filled with petty resentments. Initially, I ask forgiveness from myself. I quickly discover this does not work. I must first accept forgiveness from God. Possessing that which is freely given by God permits me to pass forgiveness on to others. I cannot live without forgiveness. Forgiveness is the determining factor that must judge all my affairs with others. The promise of forgiveness is the Fifth Step.

*Selfishness is not living as one wishes to live, it is asking others to live as one wishes to live.*
*Oscar Wilde*

## Morning Reflection 5:1

*Confidence is the only bond of friendship.*
*Publilius Syrus*

How punishment ever got mixed up with honesty is hard to say. When I walk with God there is no other way but with honesty. God cannot follow me into my fear-filled world of self-delusion. The worst that can happen to me is death. In death I will find either another life or peaceful non-existence. If I am headed for peaceful non-existence, then the most death can do for me is take me out of whatever misery I am feeling.

If, on the other hand, I experience another life after death then the question becomes, "What kind of life will it be?" Will it seem better, worse or the same? The answer to that question must have something to do with the quality of my current life. This brings me back to the point of embracing my own forgiveness.

The one overwhelming fact in the Fifth Step is I am not God. My attempts at playing God have come up short. My attempts at creating gods, whether they be other people, worldly possessions, or institutions, have left me empty and despairing. In Step Five I come face to face with my humanness. I am an everyday person with all the characteristics of common folk. Try as I will to be special and unique, the end product of my actions is quite similar to that of the fellow next door.

I share with another my Fifth Step; I drag up all sorts of dark secrets. I find out there is nothing special about my tales. In accepting my alcoholism, I come face to face with human characteristics. I have flaws, bits and pieces of character that expose themselves in ways harmful to me. These character defects are illuminated in my Fifth Step.

*A man who doesn't trust himself can never really trust anyone else.*
*Cardinal De Retz*

## Morning Promise 5:2

*It is easier to forgive an enemy than to forgive a friend.*
*William Blake*

There is a more serious side to the promise of forgiveness. The promise I am freely given, by virtue of the fact that I am loved by God, is a promise that must be extended to others. I cannot withhold that which I have been freely given. I must pass on forgiveness to receive recovery. Where there is forgiveness, there is no room for resentment. The promise is that I will have an endless supply of forgiveness I can pass to others. The promise is simple. I am forgiven, and I can forgive.

*Forgive us our debts, as we forgive our debtors.*
*Bible*

## Morning Reflection 5:2

*Be ye kind one to another, tenderhearted, forgiving one another, even as God for Christ's sake hath forgiven you.*
*Bible*

I see in my Fifth Step just where my flaws have hurt others. I see where I need forgiveness. I see where these flaws have come between me and my Higher Power. Nowhere have I seen a need for punishment. Punishment is dealt me by being born as a human being with character defects. I have caused hurt; I have felt pain because I am a human being.

The promise in Step Five is forgiveness. I know a new freedom that comes from learning I have been forgiven by God. My Higher Power is not lying in the background ready to pounce on me and punish me for being who I am. God is forever with me, ready to love me just as soon as I am ready to let go of the pain and suffering of my own making.

The secret revealed in the promise of forgiveness of Step Five is that I am more than just a human being. I am the child of a creator. I did not create myself. All my tampering and adjusting has produced only a poorer life than the one planned for me.

I want forgiveness so I can have the life into which I was born. I have been forgiven from God and can move into the future as a whole and complete man. This does not remake the past, nor does it mean that I have no work in front of me.

There is still that resentment I have been harboring for my boss of ten years ago. I find trusting anyone a difficult assignment. The Fifth Step does not wash away the work of cleaning up the wreckage of the past. What it does is give me the opportunity to clean up the past.

I want to continue to talk with God. I have found protection in all matters that face me. I find myself nudging toward the notion that if I am going to be in a relationship with God for all eternity, then it should be a good relationship.

I am begging for forgiveness at the end of my Fifth Step, and to me forgiveness is freely given. It is for me to simply and gratefully accept this forgiveness.

*We all like to forgive, and we all love best not those who offend us least, not those who have done most for us, but those who make it most easy for us to forgive them.*
*Samuel Butler*

## Morning Promise 5:3

*Sometimes even to live is an act of courage.*
*Seneca*

There is nothing in this world that can conquer a person who has taken unto themselves forgiveness! Nothing now! Nothing ever! What accounts for the stories of strength we hear from men and women who have been in recovery for years? They describe life at the bottom of the barrel, how they lost everything. Then like a miracle and by virtue of working the Steps of A.A., they utterly and completely change. They seize something about themselves, about God, and become people of stature and wisdom. I believe it is forgiveness they seize. What we find in recovery is the power of the promise. When forgiveness is embraced, what fills our empty spaces is self-esteem.

*It is a brave act of valour to contemn [despise] death; but where life is more terrible than death, it is then the truest valour to dare to live.*
*Sir Thomas Browne*

## Morning Reflection 5:3

*To every thing there is a season, and a time to every purpose under the heaven.*
*Bible, Ecclesiastes 3:1*

There is great peace and serenity in having the past stamped "approved." I feel like a gigantic exhalation of stale air has just left my body. When I was beaten and dying, I did not experience a calm serenity in death. I was trapped in hurt and self-loathing. My soul was screaming, "Don't die now, don't die now!"

My spirit knew what my mind did not. I was running on fear, and the fueling of that fear with alcohol was driving me to hell. The life I experienced in the days leading up to my assault was anything but peaceful. It was filled with torment and anguish. I was engulfed in despair. My spirit ached to be out of that life and into another, where it could experience the healing presence of God.

Yet when it came time to die, my spirit knew that it was a part of me and I was a part of it. Somehow to have died then would have been a tragic mistake. It was not the appointed hour; Washington D.C. was not the appointed place. My spirit knew it had to keep my body alive. There was unfinished business to take care of before I could die.

I cannot tell you what goes on after a person dies; I don't know. I did not see a white light. I did not see those that went before, beckoning me forward. I did not review my personal history. I can only say I experienced terror, so frightening that it kept me breathing just enough to stay alive.

I did not want to die at a time when I was fearful, guilt-ridden, lost. My glimpse of what lies beyond was not calming. It was not the peaceful tranquility of nothingness.

When I left my body, I was frightened beyond comprehension. To find myself locked in that state of being for eternity would be worse than death. The facts are there for me to see. The doctors and medical technicians had no idea how I lived through that assault. I should have died. I did not. Why? The policemen who found me had no idea why they just happened to pull up beside my body at 5:00 a.m. in a place they never visited. Why? I know why. They were instructed to do so.

Why I am living had something to do with the vitality of the spirit and its connections to a greater Power. My spirit knew damn well that it was living outside the realm of forgiveness. It was chained to the past and the actions of a man who knew no Higher Power. My spirit understood that to die without experiencing forgiveness would mean no light.

*Forgiveness is the answer to the child's dream of a miracle by which what is broken is made whole again, what is soiled is again made clean.*
*Dag Hammarskjold*

## Morning Promise 5:4

*Valour lies just half-way between rashness and cowheartedness.*
*Cervantes*

If only the world would embrace the forgiveness that is open to those of us in recovery. How long would there be the struggle between nations? Could the political turmoil in some countries endure? The promise of forgiveness is like a sign of unconditional surrender of man to God. Man wins by surrendering. The principal of winning through losing is the secret of success. The promise of forgiveness is the hope that life can be different. We no longer have to be in an endless struggle. We can have faith in this forgiveness. Perhaps if we live as those forgiven, others will follow. Perhaps the world is changed one soul at a time.

*Faith embraces many truths which seem to contradict each other.*
*Pascal*

## Morning Reflection 5:4

*Until the day of his death, no man can be sure of his courage.*
*Jean Anouilh*

I have since come to see the meaning in the words the nun shared with me as I awoke from my coma. She said, "Follow the light. If the light goes left, follow it left. If it goes right, follow it right. But remember always, follow the light." The only way to get to the light was through forgiveness. You can't follow light that isn't there.

Step Five opens up to me the illuminating lustre of forgiveness. Once I embrace forgiveness, I live in perpetual light. Once I embrace forgiveness, I can die in perpetual light. I no longer have to fear death because I take my light with me.

Step Five shows me where it was I fell into darkness. It shows how I fell repeatedly into the same dark pit. It also reveals the way out. Step Five allows me to hear my own voice say the words I admit out loud. I might as well scream it from the rooftops. I am not living a secret anymore. I clearly see where I have been. I have dug out the darkness from all corners of my life. I am letting the light in. I am ready to embrace my life as forgiven and loved by God.

Forgiveness is the promise of perpetually being on the winning team. My ego becomes proportional to the world around me. I don't need to fight with everything for position. I have courage to be who I am and kindness to let others be who they are. I live and let live.

The promise of forgiveness leads me into the ensuing Steps like a lighthouse leads a ship away from trouble. I have a beacon upon which I can set my course. I have the secret of how to resuscitate a suffocating spirit. The promise of forgiveness opens up the possibility of change and rebirth.

*The coward calls the brave man rash, the rash man calls him coward.*
*Aristotle*

# STEP SIX

Were entirely ready to have God remove all these defects of character.

## Evening Prayers and Reflections for Freedom

## Morning Promises and Reflections of Purity

## Evening Prayer 6:1

*Love, all alike, no season knows, nor clime, nor hours, age, months, which are the rags of time.*
*John Donne*

**O Thou Who Sets Me Free,** when I was younger, I wanted to be free from school, free from my parents, free from authority, free from having to work for a living. I spent years scheming to be free. I believed the fewer responsibilities I had, the freer I was. I drank to be free of reality. One day I awoke from a blackout with nothing, absolutely nothing: alienated from my family, my business bankrupt, my wife gone, living in my mother's house in the room I grew up in. I contemplated how I was finally free. All the years of striving, clawing, drinking and dreaming had brought me to this point of complete freedom. Oh, God, how I wanted at that moment to be free of my freedom. Amen.

*Never love with all your heart, It only ends in aching.*
*Countee Cullen*

## Evening Reflection 6:1

*Love is Immortality.*
*Emily Dickinson*

I am ready to cross over into a new world. I feel a lot like Dorothy in the "Wizard of Oz." Dorothy seemed to be searching for something her whole life. I too was looking for some way to fit in. Every new person, new job, new car, new book just didn't quite fit; or I did not fit them. I came to believe I was born to be unhappy. Ultimately I turned to my compulsions to find any sort of happiness.

What began as brief excursions into ecstasy ended up as extended visits to hell. I was swept away like Dorothy was. Dorothy ended up in the Land of Oz. I ended up an alcoholic.

Dorothy had to become willing to live her real life. She needed a journey to discover a reason to live her life. If something had not intervened, who knows, maybe this Kansas girl would never have found a way to live with Auntie Em, Toto, and the rest of the gang on the farm. In a sense, we all have a Kansas farmhouse we are running from.

Dorothy heard there was someone who could help her get back to Kansas. She wanted to go back. She hadn't figured out why she wanted to go back; she just knew that she did. She had to find a wizard, the Wizard of Oz, in the town of Oz at the end of the Yellow Brick Road.

It is not hard to see that the fear of not going home compelled Dorothy to take the first step on the Yellow Brick Road. She knew she was powerless over her situation. She, of her own accord, could not find a way back home. Either she took her first step or she would forever have to live with Munchkins.

She looked around at those strange little people and figured Munchkinland was not for her. She took her first step. Along the way she met other people who had never heard of Kansas. Externally she had very little in common with them. Internally, she was like them exactly. They had precisely the same problems she had had in Kansas. The Scarecrow didn't like the mind he had; Dorothy didn't like hers. The Lion didn't like the character he was born with; neither did Dorothy. The Tin Man didn't like his heart; neither did Dorothy. All of of them disliked their situations and desperately wanted to do something about changing their lives.

So if Dorothy could go home, her life would change; if the Scarecrow could get a brain, his life would change; if the Lion could get courage, his life would change; if the Tin Man could get a heart, his life would change. All these needy creatures needed a change. Each admitted they could not effect a change themselves, each admitted they were utterly powerless over their problems, but there was a power greater than themselves that could help them. That power was called the Wizard of Oz.

However, to get to Oz, they had to take certain steps. These steps could be found along the Yellow Brick Road. They all were willing to go to any lengths to find what they were looking for. They elected to take the journey together, each having a different need, but each having a similar situation of powerlessness.

How do we know they were entirely ready to have these defects of character removed? They became willing to have someone, somewhere, remove them. They came to a point where they saw that life was not worth living with these character defects. They could have stayed where they were and hoped Oz would come to them. They could have stayed where they were and tried to fix each other. They could have tried to borrow what they did not have from one another. They decided instead to take the steps down the

Yellow Brick Road. They were off to see the Wizard, the wonderful wizard of Oz, because, because, because . . . .

*Love, with very young people, is a heartless business. We drink at that age from thirst, or to get drunk; it is only later in life that we occupy ourselves with the individuality of our wine.*
*Isak Dinesen*

## Evening Prayer 6:2

*Where there is no love there is no sense either.*
*Dostoevsky*

**O Most Merciful God,** now that I am packed and ready for this journey, I find myself strangely silent. I should be welcoming the opportunity to be born anew, yet I am not. I found myself walking by the railroad tracks the other day. I noticed an old fellow with a quart of wine in his hand running up to one of the empty boxcars. He was ready to jump into the boxcar and ride it to wherever it was going. He obviously had nothing more than what he was wearing. For a split second, I found myself thinking, "You lucky son of a gun." That's right! You lucky son of a gun. My role model from my old life emerged for what it was -- a hobo wino. I always claimed I wanted to be the leader of the free world. This was all a lie. My goal in life was to become a hobo wino. Well, I almost got my wish. Thank You, God, for clearing up this little misunderstanding between me and myself. Amen.

*In order to love simply, it is necessary to know how to show love.*
*Dostoevsky*

## Evening Reflection 6:2

*Love is all we have, the only way that each can help the other.*
*Euripides*

Dorothy and her friends had no idea what was in store for them on the Yellow Brick Road. The road was not straight; it was filled with treacheries, dangers, diversions and troubles. The Yellow Brick Road was a dangerous place to be. If they did not stick together, they would surely be bushwhacked and thrown off their course.

The questions they would ask a thousand times along the route would be, "Am I really willing to go to any lengths to have this defect in me remedied? Am I really willing to endure this journey to find a way back home?" The answer came back, "Yes."

When individual resolve would wane, one of the others would pick up leadership. They supported each other. They encouraged each other to keep on the journey, keep moving down the Yellow Brick Road.

They would have to do things to get to Oz they never dreamed possible. They began to see that if each one did not make it, nobody could make it. They found themselves caring about the group. The four of them became as one. They knew they had to stay unified. The Tin Man was called on to do things that required great heart along the way. He was called on to show passion and love. He forgot he had no feelings. He discovered in his willingness to participate in the journey that when heart was needed, it was given to him.

The Scarecrow discovered he was called on to calculate how to get through difficult obstacles along the way, and these calculations required the use of his brain. He mastered each one; and without the Scarecrow's reasoning ability, the journey could not have been made.

The Lion had courage and character throughout the trip to Oz. He had to be reminded of it on occasion; but when it was asked for, he delivered. The miracle is plain for us to see. It is not draped in mysticism or magic. The requests that were to be made of the great Oz were answered along the way. It was in action that freedom was found and prayers answered.

These four found what they were looking for on the Yellow Brick Road. This small band with defective characters found their answer in their willingness to have their defects removed. The willingness to find an answer produced an answer.

*The richest love is that which submits to the arbitration of time.*
*Lawrence Durrell*

## Evening Prayer 6:3

*Resolve to perform what you ought. Perform without fail what you resolve.*
*Benjamin Franklin*

**O Great Trailmaster,** I am enjoying my trip on the wagon train to the Promised Land. Thank you for the wonderful friends you have put in my life. At one time, I guarded my solitary independence from people. That, I thought, was true freedom. Radical individualism was only the freedom to be shackled to my own small insignificant world. The freedom to be part of a spiritual fellowship and to serve the needs of others opens up a world of new opportunities. I must confess, God, that I am utterly shocked to discover that freedom comes in the midst of obedience to Your will. The more obedient I am to life and the responsibilities of living, the more free I am. I never thought this could be so, yet it is; it is. Amen.

*He that hath love in his breast hath spurs in his sides.*
*English Proverb*

## Evening Reflection 6:3

*Nothing is impossible to a willing heart.*
*R.D. Hicks*

There is a profound truth we learn from our Wizard of Oz friends. Their long-sought answers emerged when they faced their fears. The Scarecrow had a brain all along. The Tin Man had a heart all along. The Lion had courage all along. Fear kept them from using what they already had.

When the mission became getting the four of them to Oz, fear dissolved. Because they started together, stayed together, fought together, fear was conquered. It is probably true that individually they could not have made it to Oz. Individually, they would have believed the voices that told them they were stupid, cowardly, heartless, homeless people.

In their willingness to go to whatever lengths necessary to find what they were looking for, they found their hearts' desires.

Step Six is the Step of freedom. I declare my independence from the shackles of fear that have so paralyzed my development. Dorothy's sobering experience in the Land of Oz gave her freedom to be precisely who she was. She wanted to experience something special in getting her wish. She wanted the Wizard to be the great and omnipotent Oz. She wanted the drama of a special answer to her prayers.

The answer was so simple. If someone had told her the answer in Munchkinland, she would not have believed. She had no tools to believe in anything but her problems. The journey on the Yellow Brick Road with the Lion, the Tin Man and the Scarecrow gave her the answer to her prayer. She found out the secret.

The great Oz was not great, and he had no wizardly answers. In fact, as a wizard, he was a complete failure; but he *was* a great sponsor, a great friend. He had travelled the Yellow Brick Road himself. He had years on the Oz program and knew where the road led.

*Sudden resolutions, like the sudden rise of the mercury in the barometer, indicate little else than the changeableness of the weather.*
*Julius Charles Hare and Augustus William Hare*

## Evening Prayer 6:4

*He only earns his freedom and existence who daily conquers them anew.*
*Goethe*

**O Great Leader Of Lost Causes,** is freedom really wrapped up in a journey? There is a story about Gandhi, who took off one day from a village. As he walked out into the desert, a great band of people began to follow. They assumed the Mahatma was embarking on a great and glorious freedom march. Soon thousands of people were following him. The political leaders who were using Gandhi as the symbol for independence began to scheme how they could use Gandhi's walk across India as a mobilizing event for Indian independence. They constructed an elaborate plan. As Gandhi continued the walk, all the newspapers around the world picked up the story. The world was abuzz, wondering what would happen. Then Gandhi abruptly stopped. He turned around and headed back to the village from which he started his trek. The political leaders came to him and pleaded that he continue his walk. He couldn't stop now; India's freedom depended on him. Gandhi told them, "Freedom is not going somewhere. It is not a destination. Freedom is the journey. You all need to walk more. I intend to exercise my freedom and walk on back to the village. Care to join me?" Of course they all did. This, O God, is what it is like following you. Amen.

*The moment the slave resolves that he will no longer be a slave, his fetters fall. He frees himself and shows the way to others. Freedom and slavery are mental states. Mohandas K. Gandhi*

## Evening Reflection 6:4

*The history of the world is none other than the progress of the consciousness of freedom.*
*Hegel*

The Wizard of Oz was quite a sponsor. He had worked at his program and helped Dorothy and the others with theirs. Oz was freedom. Through willingness, the four travelers endured all the trials of the Yellow Brick Road. Through willingness, all their requests were granted.

There is a simple truth concerning answers to petitionary prayers. First, I need ears that hear; second, eyes that see; third, a heart that feels; fourth, a mind that thinks. Without these faculties, my prayers cannot help but fall on silence. It is never the case that I have no faculties to receive answers; it is always the case that something blocks my ability to use them. Once the blocks are removed I can have prayers that receive answers.

Dorothy got her channels clear when she decided to travel the Yellow Brick Road. She learned that home was where her heart was. She learned to love, to live; she was free to be Dorothy. She grew up. Her transforming journey to Oz and her triumphant return to Kansas symbolize rebirth.

Step Six is willingness to live freely. It is living first. It is stepping out into life and knowing there are fellow travelers on whom I can rely. I live as one whose freedom is bound by only my imagination. I find in being willing to have freedom, what tripped me up before is taken away.

The character defects that plagued me in the past disappear. Something is done for me that I could not do for myself. When I am living I am not searching. The secret is in living. The secret is found on the Yellow Brick Road. The secret is not Oz, but the Journey to Oz.

The life of my dreams is found in the living of today. The only difference between Kansas and the Land of Oz is three taps of the heels and the desire to be home. The key to the removal of character defects is in loving the life I have been so graciously given to live.

*We have confused the free with the free and easy.*
*Adlai Stevenson*

## Morning Promise 6:1

*Extreme hopes are born of extreme misery.*
*Bertrand Russell*

The promise of purity is assured by my unconditional surrender. I viewed surrender as humiliating, mortifying and deadly, very much like being executed. I have no hope until I take the step which is beyond quitting. I surrender. I unconditionally surrender. It is with this final surrender that I am made ready for the real victory in life.

*Hope is an echo, hope ties itself yonder, yonder.*
*Carl Sandburg*

## Morning Reflection 6:1

*True hope is swift and flies with swallow's wings; Kings it makes gods, and meaner creatures kings.*
*Shakespeare*

Purity of heart -- the very words sound clean. I have willed so much misery into my life. How can I receive purity of heart after a lifetime of living in shadows?

The key is my willingness to have God remove my defects. The way to use the key is to start living my Third Step decision. I have cleared my own path in my Fourth and Fifth Steps. I see quite clearly where I have been. I feel the power of the Force in my life that keeps me sober on a daily basis. I have embraced my forgiveness and now stand at the point where all things begin. I have purged the secrets of the past; I have cleared out the clutter from days, months, years gone by.

The promise is that I can move into the future with purity. If I become entirely ready, I am given purity. I must know with certainty that what God has done to my powerlessness over alcohol, he can do with my defects of character. I am sober on a daily basis. Each day that goes by when I have not touched a drop of alcohol, I have acted with purity.

My motives and actions have merged into a spiritual state where there are no shades of truth. I begin to experience days when I do not harken to my defects at all. Motive and action merge into a single action. I look at that day as a gift from God. I find in the entirety of my willingness pristine purity.

*Hope springs eternal in the human breast: man never is, but always to be blest.*
*Alexander Pope*

## Morning Promise 6:2

*Even now I am full of hope, but the end lies in God.*
*Pindar*

The promise of purity is a radical change in perspective, a process of becoming increasingly more open-minded. I have fewer prejudices. I don't feel compelled to judge everyone and everything that crosses my path. I live and let live. I know I do not know it all; in fact, I know very little. I rely on my Higher Power for knowledge. The promise of purity allows me to stop kicking religion. I no longer slander or belittle people who subscribe to different metaphors of expressing their own trust in a Higher Power. I watch a T.V. evangelist baptising a person in a big tub of water. I remember the scorn I once heaped upon such scenes. I think, "Now I know what this baptism stuff is all about." I feel brand new myself, washed clean, pure as a baby. Steps Four and Five were my baptism. The purity of Step Six opens me up to the possibility of a truly religious life.

*When he has no lust, no hatred, a man walks safely among the things of lust and hatred.*
*Bhagavadgita*

## Morning Reflection 6:2

*The sun, though it passes through dirty places, yet remains as pure as before.*
*Francis Bacon*

Step Six feels like being born again, as Dorothy was born again in Munchinkland. She could do in the world of the Munchkins what she could not do five minutes before she was swept out of Kansas.

I am actually able to complete projects, where before, all my measures in life were halfhearted. It is difficult to embrace this fact about the Sixth Step. I cannot believe I am not permanently damaged goods. The truth of the matter is I never was damaged goods.

I fight this belief like Dorothy had to fight the wicked witch. The witch knew that Dorothy possessed her freedom, but Dorothy did not know it. She hadn't had time yet to live her freedom. She didn't entirely find out until she made it to Oz.

The wicked witch wanted to take Dorothy's freedom from her. She wanted Dorothy to fear again. While Dorothy feared, she would never be free. The wicked witch knew this. So all along the Yellow Brick Road, the witch created obstacles to make Dorothy afraid. Once Dorothy was paralyzed with fright, she would no longer be free.

You see, Dorothy had to use her feet to claim her freedom. She had to walk the Yellow Brick Road. There could be no going home unless she stepped one foot in front of the other, down that road.

When Dorothy first entered Munchkinland, her house fell on the other wicked witch. That witch had misused her freedom, denying liberty to people she could have served. Freedom is a powerful gift. When it is misused, it has a way of coming back at you. That poor witch lost her life to her misuse of freedom.

Dorothy discovered that the symbol of freedom could be found in the slippers she wore on her journey to Oz. She met the good witch, her guardian angel, who became Dorothy's temporary sponsor until she met the wonderful wizard. The good witch gave Dorothy clear instructions on what to do. She told Dorothy to remember to keep those slippers on her feet, to hold on to the symbol of her freedom. Those slippers would be an ever present reminder to go the entire journey, the entire route of the Yellow Brick Road. They would remind her of her readiness to be a new Dorothy.

The witch whispered in Dorothy's ear that others had used those very same slippers to get to Oz, and they never failed to find their way home. Or she could stay just where she was. In that case she would not need the slippers.

The wicked witch wanted them and would go to any lengths to get them. She had evil plans for her freedom; she knew its power and planned to misuse it.

Dorothy had to be very careful because the minute she faltered in her decision, the moment she became a slave to the old Dorothy, she would lose her freedom. The shoes would be taken by the evil witch. Purity was

Dorothy's promise. As long as she lived her life one day at a time, continued her journey to Oz, she would be granted freedom from all the turmoil that surrounded her life. She would find new trials and tribulations, to be sure. But these would not harm her. She was totally protected.

*My strength is as the strength of ten, because my heart is pure.*
*Alfred, Lord Tennyson*

## Morning Promise 6:3

*We should not let our fears hold us back from pursuing our hopes.*
*John F. Kennedy*

Chastity is the purity of heart to will one thing. I have to remind myself to be chaste at all times. I must neither think too much nor rationalize at all. The inner workings of my heart will always tell me the truth. A conscious contact with a Higher Power is a moment by moment connection with this inner sense. I must diligently practice to listen. My mind must be turned down -- not turned off, but turned down, so it does not scream at me all the time. The deep underlayer of the heart will send me the messages I am looking for. My chastity is wrapped up in heeding what I hear.

*Strong hope is a much greater stimulant of life than any single realized joy could be.*
*Nietzsche*

## Morning Reflection 6:3

*Just as dumb creatures are snared by food, human beings would not be caught unless they had a nibble of hope.*
*Petronius*

Dorothy made her decision that this unknown Road was better than any other road she had been on. So she took off down the Yellow Brick Road, her freedom secured, pure in heart and ready to find a way home.

Steps Four and Five revealed a way to cleanse my soul and my heart. I found a way to receive God's forgiveness for all that went before. I point myself in the direction of the future and seize the freedom to be a new person. This new person has exactly the same situation as before, but a new pair of eyes with which to see it.

I discover in the promise of purity of heart that there is no place for lying, for cheating, for chipping away the truth. The instincts that ran rampant within me are inappropriate. I discover that as I have decided to live in the midst of a Higher Power, deceitful things are not welcome.

I feel a new respect for myself. I want things that will not hurt me. I want things for other people that will not hurt them. I choose to be a positive influence.

I find comfort in letting go of pain, misery and guilt. I dream and plan events that will enrich me. I am more comfortable with a smile than a frown. I recover a long-lost sense of humor. I am a newcomer, but it doesn't bother me. My self no longer needs to be a know-it-all.

I feel I have hardly begun to grow, yet I have seen more growth in the short time I have been on the journey than ever before. Can it possibly continue? I wonder what it means to be "entirely ready." Does it mean absolutely, completely, without fail ready?

Can there be room for questions at all? How will I know if I am entirely ready? If I behave like someone who is ready, then will I be ready? All these questions make my feet sweat, but I must remember what the good witch told Dorothy. Keep those slippers on! Follow the Yellow Brick Road! When Dorothy questioned her readiness and what it would mean to be entirely ready, the good witch said, "Get on that road and begin to move those feet one in front of the other." It doesn't make any difference how many questions I have.

What makes a difference is keeping my shoes on and using those shoes to walk down the road. I do not think my way pure. I do think my way into trouble. I live my way into readiness; I live my way into purity. I live daily; I die daily. My freedom is a state of being, not a state of mind.

*In the history of thought and culture the dark nights have perhaps in some ways cost mankind less grief than the false dawns, the prison houses in which hope persists less grief than the Promised Lands where hope expires.*
*Louis Kronenberger*

## Morning Promise 6:4

*Hope is a waking dream.*
*Aristotle*

The promise of purity feels like the promise of spring. I have endured some harsh and brutal winters before I experienced the wonders of spring. In winter the trees are barren, leafless and devoid of life. In the spring, tiny buds miraculously begin to sprout, and I know new life will follow. So it is with the promise of purity. Sometimes I feel alone, naked, without hope. I experience the harshness of winter in my life. I feel depressed and abandoned. Not to worry, spring will come, new life will emerge. The promise of purity is grace does abound, spring does follow winter, life follows death.

*In the time of trouble avert not thy face from hope, for the soft marrow abideth in the hard bone.*
*Hafiz*

## Morning Reflection 6:4

*Hope is a strange invention - a Patent of the Heart - in unremitting action yet never wearing out.*
*Emily Dickinson*

God walks with free people because free people walk with God. The freedom of entire readiness is claimed each morning. I learn to thank God on my knees. I claim my forgiveness as a child of God, and I give thanks for this new life. The truth has set me free one more day. I can live this day with the purity of heart of a newborn baby.

Dorothy clicked her heels together three times just as she was instructed. She was given the eyes to see the victory she had been living. Auntie Em, Toto, and all the farmhands were all there in Kansas just being themselves. The farm was the same - the nasty neighbor, the bad weather- everything as it had been. Yes, it was all the same but Dorothy was brand-new. She had shed the shackles of a life lived in fear, anger and guilt. She was free from her past. Her future was open and waiting for her.

I wonder what happened to Dorothy. Did she remember the Yellow Brick Road? Did she keep in touch with her home group, the Tin Man, the Lion and the Scarecrow? Did she keep her slippers on? What about Oz? Did she remember all the wonderful secrets she learned from the wizard? Is she staying away from slippery places where she might lose her slippers?

I don't know what Dorothy remembers, but I will not forget her.

*There is nothing so well known as that we should not expect something for nothing - but we all do and call it Hope.*
*Edgar Watson Howe*

# STEP SEVEN

Humbly asked Him to remove our shortcomings.

## Evening Prayers and Reflections for Humility

## Morning Promises and Reflections of Love

## Evening Prayer 7:1

*Everyone thinks that all the bells echo his own thoughts.*
*German Proverb*

**O Anonymous One,** I am amazed I can utter a prayer for humility. My whole life has been building my ego. I have been told to be proud of myself, to depend on myself. I have used people to help pump me up like a balloon. Then something or someone pricks my ego and the balloon pops. I cannot place my trust in myself. I want a normal ego, one that fits my *exact* size. Amen.

*Every cock is proud on his own dunghill.*
*Thomas Fuller*

## Evening Reflection 7:1

*Half of the harm that is done in this world is due to people who want to feel important.*
*T.S. Eliot*

There is a saying there are but two routes to humility: one by way of wisdom, the other by way of humiliation. Humility opposes ego. My ego has always placed itself in the middle of all my endeavors. It is a master of many voices. It whispers to me like a child that needs attention. It romances me like a beautiful woman convincing me to lavish it with attention. It becomes a bigot anytime its territory is threatened. My ego can be an intellectual snob, convincing me that my opinions are superior. It can be a power-driven dictator screaming, "Either my way or the highway." My ego believes everyone places the same value on it that it places on itself. It believes it is God.

*The turtle lays thousands of eggs without anyone knowing, but when the hen lays an egg, the whole country is informed.*
*Malay Proverb*

## Evening Prayer 7:2

*Too humble is half proud.*
*Yiddish Proverb*

**O Merciful One**, in my prayer for humility there is an end to striving. I have spent my life trying to become someone special. Steps Four and Five have given me a handle to end this circular journey. The process of self-development finally begins. When I stand before You in humility, You lead me with Your will and I subject my will to Yours. I no longer build monuments to myself. I participate in a greater plan, one which will benefit others and ultimately make me happiest. Thank You. Amen.

*The sons of Adam are formed from dust; if not humble as the dust, they fall short of being men.*
*Sa'di*

## Evening Reflection 7:2

*Man was created on the sixth day so that he could not be boastful, since he came after the flea in the order of creation.*
*Haggadah*

In my younger days, there was a famous ventriloquist named Edgar Bergen. His partner was Charlie McCarthy. Charlie, of course, was a dummy; but Mr. Bergen was such a good entertainer I was convinced Charlie was a real person.

I wasn't alone in my belief. People all over the country wrote to Charlie, asking him for help and advice. There were Charlie McCarthy dolls, masks, cartoons. To all outward appearances, the dummy had a life of its own without Edgar Bergen.

Of course this wasn't true. But what if Charlie McCarthy had thought he was alive and running the show? He might have reasoned something like this:

"All these people love me. I must be a very important person. I'm the star of the show. Who is this Edgar Bergen to be telling me what to say and do?"

Charlie has forgotten his Higher Power. He has begun to play God.

*We come nearest to the great when we are great in humility.*
*Rabindranath Tagore*

## Evening Prayer 7:3

*Humility has the toughest hide.*
*Nietzsche*

**Dear Lord Of History,** I often wonder how it is I've turned up in a certain spot. I'll be hurting in a particular way and hear someone say something that addresses my exact situation. Or, in turn, I will say something that addresses someone else's exact situation. Very often my phone will ring, and by some coincidence a friend will call to tell me something that answers a question that formerly seemed unsolvable to me. Now it seems that a situation does not occur that does not appear to be the workings of divine providence. I used to think of such events as freak happenings, the proverbial luck of the draw. Now I understand all things in life have a purpose. I may not understand the purpose, but there assuredly is one. Please keep my eyes clear and my ears open. Amen.

*The fuller the ear is of rice-grain, the lower it bends, empty of grain, it grows taller and taller.*
*Malay Proverb*

## Evening Reflection 7:3

*There is no humiliation for humility.*
*Joseph Roux*

As time went on, Charlie became more and more certain he was in control of his life. But how could he tell Edgar he wasn't needed any more, that his role was outdated, and Charlie wanted to go on alone?

Then something happened. Edgar Bergen decided to retire. Charlie was ecstatic. Now he wouldn't be held back any more. He could be all he wanted to be -- the greatest dummy in creation!

The big day came. Mr. Bergen was going to announce his retirement. The studio set was decorated with flowers and banners. People called from all over the world with warm messages of appreciation. Charlie was dressed in a tuxedo. Edgar wore an old beat-up corduroy jacket.

Charlie knew exactly what he was going to say. He had decided his scope was too small as an entertainer; he planned to announce his candidacy for President of the United States. America needed his guidance.

The broadcast began and Edgar spoke. "Ladies and gentlemen, boys and girls, this is Edgar Bergen. You all know me as the voice of Charlie McCarthy. I want to thank you for all the wonderful years you've given me. If Charlie could talk, he'd tell you he loves you all."

Charlie tried to interrupt to tell the audience his great plan, but nothing happened. Edgar continued, "It's time for Charlie and me to retire and leave the stage to new entertainers. We've had years of your friendship and support. Without you we would have been nothing. You gave us life. We humbly thank you. Charlie, say goodbye to all our friends."

Charlie opened his mouth to tell everyone he was going to be President. What came out was, "Goodbye, and thank you all." Charlie had just met his Higher Power once again.

*There must be feelings of humility, not from nature, but from penitence, not to rest in them, but to go on to greatness.*
*Pascal*

## Evening Prayer 7:4

*It is a bitter dose to be taught obedience after you have learned to rule.*
*Publilius Syrus*

**O Master Of All That Will Be**, if I am to be a fool, let me be a fool for You. I, like Charlie, am a dummy with my stuffing shaken loose. I have lost interest in things that create pain for me. I want things that bring me peace and serenity. Nothing can rattle me when I am in close contact with You. Please accept my good faith decision to render obedience to You. I am a child. I may always be a child. Please take me into Your confidence and allow me to participate with You in building the future. Amen.

*A man who has humility will have acquired in the last reaches of his beliefs the saving doubt of his own certainty.*
*Walter Lippmann*

# Evening Reflection 7:4

*The eagle never lost so much time as when he submitted to learn of the crow.*
*William Blake*

Humility is not a concession I make to God. It is the conscious recognition that I am a visitor to this world at the invitation of God. Humility has two predominant characteristics: a reverence for the power that sustains me, and absolute honesty with myself. I work at telling the truth every day. I let each day remind me of the glory and majesty of God. Defects of character become manageable when I am reverent and honest. I no longer attempt to control other people. I see God's signature on all of life. A clear assessment of my life quickly dispels the illusion that I am the creator of the life around me. With humility I ask only for the right things. With humility I get closer to God. My ego is cut to its proper size.

*A modest man is usually admired - if people ever hear of him.*
*Edgar Watson Howe*

## Morning Promise 7:1

*The love we give away is the only love we keep.*
*Elbert Hubbard*

The promise of love is unlike anything I could have expected. I always thought love had something to do with being loved. The state of being lovable was a quest of mine for most of my life. Whether it meant getting a better haircut, a deeper tan, a slimmer waist, or whiter teeth, love had something to do with myself. The promise in Step Seven has nothing to do with me directly. I become a receiver and giver of light, of love, of the life that moves through me. Love is not a selfish expression of fulfillment through another person; it is the radiant reward of becoming less selfish and more giving.

*Love is that condition in which the happiness of another person is essential to your own.*
*Robert A. Heinlein*

## Morning Reflection 7:1

*Though a man excels in everything, unless he has been a lover his life is lonely, and he may be likened to a jewelled cup which can contain no wine.*
*Yoshida Kenko*

As we are loved, so also is all creation loved. When I stand humble before God, freed from my defects, I feel the warmth of His love. I, nurtured by my Higher Power, can nurture others. I understand that spiritual growth and love are the same things. Love is a state of being. While I grow spiritually, I feel pain acutely. During this process I am deeply loved. When I understand how deeply I am loved and stop fighting the way I am loved, then I too can love. Step Seven's promise is love. I am a beacon, a direct reflection of the love of my Higher Power. My defects are removed so God's light might shine through me.

Love is tricky because it means so many different things. The love promised in Step Seven is that of becoming a transmitter of life. The life I have been given pours through me to others. I am not trying to *be* loving, I *am* loving. I am emitting love by being myself.

*The supreme happiness of life is the conviction that we are loved.*
*Victor Hugo*

## Morning Promise 7:2

*Love is union with somebody, or something, outside oneself, under the condition of retaining the separateness and integrity of one's own self.*
*Erich Fromm*

I have found in my promise a heart that will no longer break. I have discovered in my relationship to God a love that cannot be betrayed. I realize the truest and most unspoiled devotion I can imagine. There is a story about a mother who had just returned from a shopping trip with her baby. The child followed her mother out of the car, the emergency brake failed, the car drifted backwards, and pinned the baby under one of the tires. The mother came rushing back, took hold of the bumper and lifted the car off her child. Where the strength came from, God only knows. The promise is that God does know.

*It seems that it is madder never to abandon one's self than often to be infatuated; better to be wounded, a captive and a slave, than always to walk in armor.*
*Margaret Fuller*

## Morning Reflection 7:2

*Try to reason about love, and you will lose your reason.*
*French Proverb*

I heard the clarion call of the Peace Corps generation to change the world. I felt this call very strongly. I wanted to feed the poor, heal the sick, right all wrongs. I fancied myself a revolutionary on the side of goodness. I shared the opinion that religion was the "opiate of the masses." People, I felt, had to seize their lives and move into their future with intention. We had to build structures of care to assist the have-nots of the world. When I saw injustice, I felt it was my duty to fight it. During the sixties, I cheered every freedom march. I supported legislation to help the poor. When I witnessed the tearing down of old institutions, I applauded. The new had to be born, and I intended to be a midwife. I believed all this could be accomplished if I had discipline. Discipline was the key. The fuel for discipline was willpower. We needed to forge a common will and bend ourselves into a disciplined unit to usher in the new world.

What happened to all this willful discipline can be summed up in one word - Failure! True growth of the human spirit is a product of love, not will. He that cannot love, cannot participate in growth.

*Immature love says: "I love you because I need you." Mature love says: "I need you because I love you."*
*Erich Fromm*

## Morning Promise 7:3

*There is no harvest for the heart alone; the seed of love must be eternally resown.*
*Anne Morrow Lindbergh*

My dear aunt is a nun who for forty-plus years has spent each day caring for others. If she has not been physically involved in the care, she has been in prayer over how to care. She has concerned herself with standing before God in humility. She radiates a warmth, a love and gentleness that touches each soul she meets. A sponsor I know works as a carpenter by day. By night he works with recovering alcoholics. He changed my life with his statement, "You only hit bottom when you quit digging." He too radiates a warmth and serene confidence that touches each soul he meets. The manifestation of love is a practical, concrete manifestation of spirituality.

*There is no disguise which can hide love for long where it exists, or simulate it where it does not.*
*La Rochefoucauld*

## Morning Reflection 7:3

*It is love, not reason, that is stronger than death.*
*Thomas Mann*

While in India, I worked with a group that had its eye on helping the village poor throughout the country. Their goal was nothing less than the complete transformation of economic and social structures. My job was to attract financing for this work.

Each morning as I left on my morning calls, I passed a beggar who lay on the sidewalk next to the building where I was staying. He never left that little piece of cement. He begged for his food and smiled at everyone who went by. I did not know where he came from, whether he had a family, how he went to the bathroom, what he ate. He was just there all the time, smiling at me. I could not leave the front door without seeing this man. At first I smiled back at him and waved as I hurried off to the days' calls. He became the symbol of what I was working for.

As time wore on and my work met with less and less success, I developed a resentment for the beggar. He began to irritate me with his smile. I would mumble to myself as I passed, "Why don't you get a job?" I began to scowl at him and call him lazy. His big smile made me angry all day long. I started leaving by the back door because my resentment had grown so deep. Wherever I saw a beggar (which was everywhere) I became bitter and angry. My sense of justice and injustice turned around. I became the oppressed, the victim. I was sorry for myself. I began to hate the people, the work, the whole business of changing the world.

*Love should be practiced like Lent, secretly and dumbly.*
*Paris Leary*

## Morning Promise 7:4

*Love is the true price of love.*
*George Herbert*

The moment has come to become the self I was ordained to be, not the self of my high school dreams or the one I read about in magazines, but the real me, the essential me, presented anew, fresh, with purity and innocence, with a bright red label stamped ACCEPTED, APPROVED, READY FOR WEAR. I put myself on in a different way, with a smile on my face and love in my heart. I want good things for the world and for myself. I have cast fear away and am ready to go forth in love.

*Even as love crowns you so shall he crucify you. Even as he is for your growth so he is for your pruning.*
*Kahlil Gibran*

## Morning Reflection 7:4

*What we call love is the desire to awaken and to keep awake in another's body, heart and mind, the responsibility of flattering, in our place, the self of which we are not very sure.*
*Paul Geraldy*

As I continued my work in India, my disposition grew fouler. One day a car blocked my path into the back entry, and I was forced to go by the beggar to get into my building. This time he was not alone.

A nun was sitting on the sidewalk, with the beggar's head in her lap. He was lying there with that same smile on his face. His breathing was labored. Every so often, the Sister would lift his head up, hug him and rub his cheek. She saw me staring and smiled. The beggar saw me and smiled. Their tender looks cut me to the quick. I asked, "What are you doing, Sister?" She said, "I am caring for this man." I muttered something about a hospital and she answered, "He is dying. He needs me and I need him." I asked her if she was family. She said no. I asked her why she didn't take him to the hospital. She said again, more quietly than the first time, that he was dying. She added, "What this man needs is love. He needs to know someone loves him. I am so fortunate to be chosen to love him before he dies."

I was stunned and shaken. I got down on one knee and touched the Sister's hand where it pressed against the man's face. I could feel the heat and energy entering into him. His face glowed. His eyes pierced me. It was amazing. She was transmitting love into this man. Then he changed color, expelled a breath of air and died. He passed away in the midst of the most intense love affair I had ever witnessed. My hand fell limp. I moved away from the body and the Sister, slowly rising to my feet. The smile on the Sister's face did not change. She stared me down with her smile. Bile rose in my throat. I turned and ran. I had been exposed. I was the fraud. What moved through me was not love, it was my own ego I had been stroking all those years. I was totally lost. Somewhere I had to find a way to love.

I soon left India. My answer didn't come until I embraced Step Seven and the Promise of Love.

*A life without love, without the presence of the beloved, is nothing but a mere magic-lantern show. We draw out slide after slide, swiftly tiring of each, and pushing it back to make haste for the next.*
*Goethe*

# STEP EIGHT

Made a list of all people we had harmed, and became willing to make amends to them all.

## Evening Prayers and Reflections for Charity

## Morning Promises and Reflections of Compassion

## Evening Prayer 8:1

*Compassion for the friend should conceal itself under a hard shell.*
*Nietzsche*

**O Thou Who Forgives Everything** (even what is shelved away in my darkest hiding places), as I become more honest about my life I seem to understand other people better. That has had an effect on how I feel about myself. I no longer feel like a walking, talking basket case. Yes, God, I just feel better. For so many years I was a chronically wounded soldier. Now I am healing. I spend a lot less time licking my own wounds. I am taking a new interest in people. I actually care for others. Thank you for these changes. Amen.

*The entire world would perish, if pity were not to limit anger.*
*Seneca the Elder*

## Evening Reflection 8:1

*Verily, I do not like them, the merciful who feel blessed in their pity; they are lacking too much in shame. If I must pity, at least I do not want it known; and if I do pity, it is preferably from a distance.*
*Nietzsche*

Not long ago, I was down in a ravine behind my childhood home, walking below a bridge that spans it. I kicked at a rotting tree stump and uncovered some tiny bones. I remembered something that had happened on that bridge when I was in kindergarten. I was walking across the bridge with a kitten following me, jumping up and down as kittens do. Some older boys were trailing me, taunting me and calling me names. They came up beside me, grabbed the kitten and threw it over the bridge. I ran home in tears.

Staring at those little bones, I thought, "Maybe these are from that kitten." I found as many as I could and dug a hole and buried them. I conducted a mini-burial service. At the end of the service I asked God to forgive those bullies for their long-ago act. Then I too forgave them.

*Compassionate understanding too often buys a long-range peace with a small-change gesture - like giving a quarter to a beggar.*
*Ross Wetzsteon*

## Evening Prayer 8:2

*One cannot weep for the entire world. It is beyond human strength. One must choose.*
*Jean Anouilh*

**O God**, that Big Book has got me thinking about things differently. The way the Fourth Step questions were asked made me focus on my responsibility for certain acts. For the most part, I saw my resentments only as acts that were done *to* me. Now I see those acts as done *by* me. The book has changed how I see people I think have hurt me. I see them as people who suffer just like me. I suppose if I never considered myself human, why would I consider anyone else human? My perspective is changing as I pray for charity. I pray that I continue to own my citizenship in the human race and begin to treat other people as if they too were citizens. Amen.

*Pour not water on a drowning mouse.*
*Thomas Fuller*

## Evening Reflection 8:2

*Teach me to fell another's woe, to hide the fault I see; that mercy I to others show, that mercy show to me.*
*Alexander Pope*

In my defiant young years, I regarded the Vietnam War with contempt. I burned my draft card and refused to participate in the selective service system. After repeated efforts by the selective service system to get me to acknowledge their authority over me, I was finally pressed into action. I had to decide either to submit to the system or go to jail. I elected to do the latter. I regarded the men who served in Vietnam as cowards. I had contempt for those men. Until the Eighth Step, I had no idea that I owed amends to the men and women who served in the armed forces during the Vietnam conflict.

When the ego is used as a sword, then it leaves wounds. Wounds created in God's name are never in defense of God, only in my own name. All the time I was defending God, championing the cause of the less fortunate, I was trumpeting my own ego. Who was I to assume judgement over the men and women who went to war? How did I think I could peer into their souls and judge them patriot or traitor? I have discovered I can hate the war and love the warriors. When I am reconciled to God, I am given the heart to have charity.

Step Eight is an opportunity to draw many inner battles to a close. My list of amends includes whole eras of my life when I seemed to be fighting everybody and everything. I cannot live in a new world while I have one foot in the old. I cannot love the future while hating the past. I must close the circle. I have debts to pay, relationships to mend, apologies to make.

*Sweet mercy is nobility's true badge.*
*Shakespeare*

## Evening Prayer 8:3

*A tear dries quickly, especially when it is shed for the troubles of others.*
*Cicero*

**O Charitable One**, the Golden Rule is quite different from the one I have lived. Mine said, "Do unto others before they do it to me." Living on the offensive is wicked. For most of my life I adorned myself with the accouterments of battle, spiritually dressed like a medieval soldier. I would clank about, ready for anybody or anything that came by. Now I pray for charity. I am transparently exposed, yet more protected than I ever was with my self-made armor. I see more good than evil. I hear more praise than derision. I feel more love than hate. I am a lot lighter now. Amen.

*Though I speak with the tongues of men and of angels, and have not charity, I am become as sounding brass, or a tinkling cymbal.*
*Bible*

## Evening Reflection 8:3

*Endow the living with the tears you squander on the dead.*
*Emily Dickinson*

Charity for others cannot be real unless I have charity for myself. I must be willing to make amends to myself. Often I have played old battles back in my mind, trying to change the outcome. Each replay gives me another opportunity to curse myself. Step Eight allows me to live with charity for myself. I, too, can become the object of my affections.

The week before my father died we engaged in a fistfight, the first time I had ever struck him. Drunk, he had humiliated me in front of my best friend. I said something smart to him and he became very angry. He marched me into the garage and took off his belt as he had done on so many other occasions. This time I decided it would not happen. He raised the belt, and as he prepared to hit me, I struck him as hard as I could. Blood poured from his lip. He lunged for me and I hit him again, this time on the side of the head. He went down. I saw I had hurt him. He got to his feet and grabbed his heart, gasping for breath. I ran to him and hugged him, crying, "I'm sorry, I'm sorry, I'm sorry!" He left the garage and I did not see him again until he left on his last trip. Four days later he was dead.

I was stunned. What sank deep into me was the idea I had played a part in putting my father into the grave. For years I was plagued by the thought that Dad died in sin. If that were the case, maybe I had participated in condemning my Father to Hell for all eternity.

I never knew this was my burden until I made my list of people I had harmed. I had to put my own name on that list. I had no idea how or where I would free myself from that load of guilt.

The willingness to make amends to myself over this incident with my Father came in a walk I took many months after I had made my list. I was walking beside a cliff and was seized by what I thought was a heart attack. All the breath left my lungs. I went down on my knees. The only thing that came to my mind was I was going to meet a fate similar to my father's.

As I crouched waiting for the next blast of pain, I was engulfed in warmth. I felt the presence of my father holding me. I felt his love and tenderness.

The willingness to forgive myself for the guilt I had carried could only come from God. I have found a wonderful relationship with my father since then.

*You may regret calamities if you can thereby help the sufferer, but if you cannot, mind your own business.*
*Emerson*

## Evening Prayer 8:4

*Where Mercy, Love, and Pity dwell, there God is dwelling too.*
*William Blake*

**The prayer** of the Eighth Step is the prayer for charity. If I have come to experience my own forgiveness, if I can feel the purity of heart of being born anew, if I can touch the full force of love being transmitted through me, then and only then can I experience charity. Charity redefines for me my relationship to others. I now come to regard my fellow man with a new respect. I understand their deep connection to a Higher Power, their beloved status with God. As I walk with God, I walk with whom God walks. The Eighth Step prayer will bring me back into union with all those with whom I have become estranged. Amen.

*In necessary things, unity; in doubtful things, liberty; in all things, charity.*
*Richard Baxter*

## Evening Reflection 8:4

*Did universal charity prevail, earth would be a heaven, and hell a fable.*
*Charles Caleb Colton*

I decided the only way I could bring my resentment for the Vietnam War to a close was to make a pilgrimage to the Vietnam War Memorial in Washington D.C. I did not know what to expect. I prayed for charity on this matter and placed myself totally in the hands of my Higher Power.

I arrived at the Memorial late one night. Floodlights shone on a gigantic monolith. Before me was a wall with the names of men and women who had died in Viet Nam. The site was filled with visitors, even at that hour. Middle-aged women wept, their hands pressed up against a particular name, one hand, one name amid 54,000. The air was thick with awe. I felt humbled. Here were the collected hopes and dreams of an entire generation.

I scanned each name with tears rolling down my face. I felt I was touched by each of these souls. I asked them all for their forgiveness. I walked the entire length of the monument, thanking God for giving me the willingness to make amends to these souls.

Charity is delivered to me in bits and pieces. God's time is not my time. I must keep my candle lit so I don't miss these opportunities. When I have willingness, I prepare myself for absolution.

*In faith and hope the world will disagree, but all mankind's concern is charity.*
*Alexander Pope*

## Morning Promise 8:1

*To oblige persons often costs little and helps much.*
*Baltasar Gracian*

The promise of compassion comes with reattachment to the world. Even more important, I am reattached to my feelings about being in the world. I feel not only passion for life but empathy with life. I can receive love, and I can also give love. I remember waiting for an airplane at O'Hare Airport. There was a commotion at an adjoining gate. A plane had landed, and a group of people were waiting for someone to disembark. The group appeared to be a large family, two adults and several children, all different nationalities. A nurse came down the ramp carrying a baby and handed it to the woman waiting there. The children all squealed with joy. I walked over to see what was going on. I asked the man if all these children were his. He said yes, that he and his wife had adopted eight children and with this new baby, nine. His wife was radiant. The whole scene filled O'Hare with warmth and compassion.

*The charity that is a trifle to us can be precious to others.*
*Homer*

## Morning Reflection 8:1

*A favor well bestowed is almost as great an honor to him who confers it as to him who receives it.*
*Richard Steele*

Willingness to have my character defects removed produces within me purity of heart. I feel born anew. As I read the list of people I have harmed over my life, I am caught by one unmistakable reality: they are human beings just like me. Everything I have learned about myself I have learned about my fellow man. They suffer from their condition as I do. Everyone who ever walked the earth has had questions similar to my own. Godplaying is not unique to me. Since Adam and Eve, man has battled his desire to be God.

When I understood I was powerless over alcohol, a basic human truth was revealed. Without God I am powerless over everything. The promise of fortitude allowed me to stand erect. A Second Step prayer for belief awakened me to the possibility of living safely. I did not have to distance reality and cheat myself of the opportunity to live in the real world. When I embraced this belief I was given the promise of truth that would never let me down.

The pillar of truth is just as mighty for my neighbor as it is for me. Truth is not a spiritual requisite for only the recovering person. It exists as the bedrock upon which any fellowship with God exists. The acid test of this truth came in my Third Step, when I asked myself, could it be trusted beyond all else? Was this belief of protection and comfort in a Higher Power the most fundamental truth of all?

I answer "Yes" and embrace my Higher Power, turning over my will and life to God's care. I receive a faith that becomes a reflection of all my life's experiences. The utter submission to a Power greater than me determines all my future actions.

*Love is not love until love's vulnerable.*
*Theodore Roehke*

## Morning Promise 8:2

*We are ordinarily so indifferent to people that when we have invested one of them with possibility of giving us joy, or suffering, it seems as if he must belong to some other universe, he is imbued with poetry.*
*Marcel Proust*

Compassion promises I can lose myself in the care of something outside myself. I met a Viet Nam veteran who had lost both legs and an arm to the war. He regretted the loss of his limbs, but not the cause for which they were lost. He had decided the loss of his limbs was an acceptable price. He never allowed himself to question the truth for which he had fought. He let no one define the meaning of his life. He dared to be compassionate even if it meant fighting, even if it meant suffering. The promise of Step Eight is that I will feel so compelled with my own life.

*In one sense, the opposite of fear is courage, but in the dynamic sense the opposite of fear is love, whether this be love of man or love of justice.*
*Alan Paton*

## Morning Reflection 8:2

*'Tis never for their wisdom that one loves the wisest, or for their wit that one loves the wittiest; 'tis for benevolence and virtue and honest fondness one loves people.*
*Hester Lynch Piozzi*

I know for certain that everyone I pass on the street struggles on a daily basis with taking a relationship to a Higher Power. My 12-Step Program allows me to grow into a meaningful relationship with God. It guides me in my spiritual development. Step Four puts me to work. First I must see where I broke connection with my Higher Power. My Fourth Step lets me become fearless through my inventory. The promise of illumination clearly lights the patterns, lines and details of my personal history. I absorb the shock of this graphic illumination because I am secure in my Third Step faith. I no longer hate myself. The Fourth Step lets me re-experience my own humanity. I begin to feel compassion for myself. This is the promise of Step Eight.

*[Love is] the joy of the good, the wonder of the wise, the amazement of the gods; desired by those who have no part in him, and precious to those who have the better part in him.*
*Plato*

## Morning Promise 8:3

*Love is a naked child: do you think he has pockets for money?*
*Ovid*

The promise of compassion can be hard to live with. Often I am called on to offer a tougher kind of love. Compassion frequently is *not* a handkerchief and a shoulder to cry on. Compassion can be a kick in the backside or a slap in the face. When I lived through the loss of a significant relationship, I died inside. I thought nothing could be as brutal and cold and cruel as a divorce. I sought counseling from the wisest man I knew. I begged him to see me. I knew that if he would give me a few moments of his time he would say the things to make sense of my shattered world. The problem was we could never get together on a time. One meeting after another was cancelled. Finally after six weeks, we had lunch together. During lunch he said nothing to me about my problems. After we had finished our coffee and were ready to leave, he took my hand. He squeezed it hard and asked, "Son, have you created a resolve about your life?" Startled, I answered, "Well, yes." He said, "Then live with it." Compassion can be warm or cold, but it is always real.

*If you'd be loved, be worthy to be loved.*
*Ovid*

## Morning Reflection 8:3

*When a man is in love he endures more than at other times; he submits to everything.*
*Nietzsche*

I will transfer the compassion for myself in Steps Six and Seven to others. I feel the common link between human beings. As I feel compassion for the lost soul that was me, I feel it for the other lost souls I have met. It is clear that the common bond with my fellow man has been our alienation from God. It becomes equally clear that the bond we all have with God is that we are all equally forgiven.

Willingness to make amends does not accept excuses. Willingness to admit my part of broken relationships may not appease anger. Step Eight allows God to bring the bits and pieces together and complete the circle of life and death. Walking with God is walking with whom God walks. I can't walk with God and keep a bag over my head so nobody will recognize me.

What makes my willingness to make amends difficult is that my memory continues to deceive me. It seduces me to recall the past. It has no facility to protect me from the future. I must do my Step Eight with my soul, not my memory. My soul will direct me on the path to compassion. My soul seeks serenity and peace. It will guard me against rationalization.

*I am the least difficult of men. All I want is boundless love.*
*Frank O'Hara*

## Morning Promise 8:4

*We don't love qualities, we love persons; sometimes by reason of their defects as well as of their qualities.*
*Jacques Maritain*

The promise of compassion is like Jesus on the cross turning to the criminal who wanted to share his inventory, and reminding him he was forgiven. The man was already forgiven, but Jesus was reminding him of his forgiveness. It was for Jesus to be compassionate because it was his identity to be compassionate. The promise that I will be compassionate is a recognition that I am a changed person. Jesus, in extending his good news to the criminal, was merely being what he already was. It becomes that way with me in Step Eight. I want to make amends because it is the compassionate thing to do. I hesitate only when I ask the question, "Will it inflict harm on the other person?" Jesus saved the world by never losing sight of the individual. Even until his last breath he was compassionate about another suffering soul. Compassion lives and breathes in the mundane and particular. The promise is kept with each compassionate encounter I have.

*He that would eat of love must eat it where it hangs.*
*Edna St. Vincent Millay*

## Morning Reflection 8:4

*We are not the same persons this year as last; nor are those we love. It is a happy chance if we, changing, continue to love a changed person.*
*W. Somerset Maugham*

Memory conjures up fear, anger, dread, all the qualities of my past that plugged my channel to God. Memory replays the tape of relationships. I create excuses and reasons why I should shorten my list. My memory tolerates only small doses of willingness. Regret and guilt can collapse my efforts to find willingness. The effects of Step Three are new to me. Memory does not yet realize I have turned my will and life over to a Power greater than myself. Memory does not experience the Fortitude, Truth, Faith, Illumination, Forgiveness, Purity of Heart, Love and Compassion that move through me. The new tapes have not had time to play.

Once again, I find my mind at war with my soul. I find willingness from within my soul, speaking to me as intuition. The soul's message will keep me tuned into who I am and who I am becoming, so I don't turn around and go in the wrong direction.

Willingness is not rational; it is spiritual. The willingness to make amends to my fellow travellers is my declaration of freedom. Once again I can be a common traveller on the way, a worker among workers. Willingness allows compassion to flow through me. It transmits warmth and love into another soul. Willingness to make amends is a handshake while your eyes gleam.

Step Eight provides the promise of compassion. Compassion is the fuel that will get me back home. My list is my map of how I get there.

*To be loved means to be consumed. To love is to give light with inexhaustible oil. To be loved is to pass away, to love is to endure.*
*Rainer Maria Rilke*

# STEP NINE

Made direct amends to such people wherever possible, except when to do so would injure them or others.

## Evening Prayers and Reflections for Intercession

## Morning Promises and Reflections of Absolution

## Evening Prayer 9:1

*To love is to choose.*
*Joseph Roux*

**O Father Who Eternally Lends A Hand To The Weak,** I ask You to see me through my amends. I ask for Your intercession. There are several amends I don't know how to make. I accumulated debts I don't know how I can repay, some from many years ago. I am on the ground and making solid progress toward balancing my accounts. But my past problems feel like fire to my feet. I realize that amends are always practical and specific. I put my case before Thee in specific terms. I will create a budget that satisfies all my debts. I will stand up for my life, even if it takes the rest of it. I will be accountable. Amen.

*The repentance of man is accepted by God as virtue.*
*Voltaire*

## Evening Reflection 9:1

*Love should be a tree whose roots are deep in the earth, but whose branches extend into heaven.*
*Bertrand Russell*

My Ninth Step prayer for intercession is my re-immersion into the world. I feel like a new diver who has never been in deep water. I have been thoroughly trained for the dive but I have never actually made it. Will this equipment I am wearing really enable me to exist under water? Will oxygen be delivered each time I breathe? Will I remember to breathe through my mouth and not my nose? Will I keep calm and not hyperventilate? How will I exist in the new world I am about to enter?

The making of amends is like diving into a new environment with a different set of living conditions. I ask my Higher Power for the ability to do what's right and to protect me from all harm. I continue to fight my memory, which haunts me with past defeats. Listening to my soul is as strange as breathing through an oxygen tank. The learning process takes time. I must allow myself to be uncomfortable. New patterns are not easy.

As a diver must trust his tank, I must trust God.

I had no idea how I would ever make direct amends to the brave soldiers who fought in Viet Nam. I had to ask God to intercede on my behalf. One day I found myself having reason to go to Washington D.C. My prayers for intercession were answered when I could stand before the Viet Nam War Memorial and make my direct amends to the soldiers who died in Viet Nam. Prayers of intercession ask only for the opportunity to transmit my compassion to those whom I have harmed. The outcome of such transmissions are entirely in God's hands. I have no control over the outcome. I cannot anticipate when a relationship will be brought into full circle.

There will be those who reject my amends. The point is to act with compassion and charity, but with no expectations. I cannot know what the Divine Plan is for anyone else. My own plan is revealed one step at a time. God will intercede for me at the appropriate hour.

*The invisible path of gravity liberates the stone. The invisible slope of love liberates man.*
*Saint-Exupery*

## Evening Prayer 9:2

*It is not necessary to light a candle to the sun.*
*English Proverb*

**O Creator Of Heaven And Earth,** I ask you for a very specific favor. I need your intercession on an amends that I cannot make by myself. I was only 13 when my father died, but I harbored a terrible resentment for him. We fought, and the blows I gave him hurt him. I owe him an apology. What I thought I would do is go out to his gravesite and make my amends there. It is 27 years since he died, but hardly a week has gone by that I have not thought of my dad and that fight. I ask You to clear the slate for me. Thanks. Amen.

*We are doubly willing to jump into the water after someone who has fallen in, if there are people present who have not the courage to do so.*
*Nietzsche*

## Evening Reflection 9:2

*Kick away the ladder and one's feet are left dangling.*
*Malay Proverb*

My grandfather was my mentor in the years after my father's passing. He taught me many things about being a good person. Grandpa was an Irish immigrant, who came to America in 1910. When he left Ireland, he knew it might be many years before he could go back. Conditions in Ireland at that time were very bleak for farmers. They were not able to feed the population. There were too many people on too little land. Young men were forced to leave a country they loved because they physically could not stay. The farm was passed on to the eldest boy. The girls married, became nuns, or immigrated. The younger boys became priests or immigrated. They were frightening times. The thought of sending your children to a far-off land without the prospect of ever seeing them again was horrifying.

My grandfather often told me about his leaving. He wanted to stay and fight the British. He felt very strongly about Irish independence. He had met and fallen in love with a young woman who lived near his village. Grandpa desperately tried to find some acreage on which he and his love could settle. That was the only way he would be able to marry her. Grandpa was functionally illiterate. The school system in Ireland at the turn of the century did not take the average person beyond the sixth grade.

Time went on, and Grandpa was forced to come to terms with his situation. He must either join the priesthood or leave Ireland. The family farm was going to his brother. He took his sweetheart out one day and told her that he was leaving Ireland. He promised her he would find his way in America and send for her. They pledged their faithfulness, and Grandpa left for America. He worked in the rubber factories in Boston and the copper mines in Butte, Montana. Finally he settled in Seattle in 1912. He wrote repeatedly to his young love in County Cork, but never received a reply. In anger and frustration, he sent his final letter, telling her not to come; he had found somebody new and did not love her any more. Not long after that final letter was sent, Grandpa met and married my grandmother.

*Knowing sorrow well, I learn the way to succor the distressed.*
*Vergil*

## Evening Prayer 9:3

*One word frees us of all the weight and pain of life: That word is love.*
*Sophocles*

**O Kind And Gentle Judge,** I owe amends to myself for the years I have abused myself. If another person had treated me as I have treated myself I would have hated them. I see myself so differently now. A friend once told me if I committed suicide in the first two years of recovery, I would be killing a stranger. That is truth. My self-esteem was nonexistent. I assumed I deserved all the trouble that came my way. I was cruel to myself. I incessantly beat on myself. When I wasn't pounding away, I drank and started the whole cycle again. I refused myself joy, laughter and real friends. I chased closeness and love away from my life. I condemned myself to isolation and fear. O Lord, help me to say to this, my former life, I am profoundly sorry. My amends must allow this lowly self to stand tall again and take real pride in being Your child. I am made in your image and am to be held close as a dearly loved person. Amen.

*Base men being in love have then a nobility in their natures more than is native to them.*
*Shakespeare*

## Evening Reflection 9:3

*True love's the gift which God has given to man alone beneath the heaven.*
*Sir Walter Scott*

Grandpa loved to pass on what he believed to be ancient Celtic wisdom. I adored those sessions. My grandma would cry when he told stories. He was filled with passion for his heritage.

During these sessions he shared with me the story of his lost love. He remembered every word of his last letter to her. He could not understand how he could have been so cruel. He could not become reconciled to it as the action of a young man desperate to be with the one he loved. When I asked him why he hadn't taken steps to apologize or make amends, he would shrug his shoulders and say the time was never quite right. I think he intended to make his amends personally, but it never came to pass.

My last visit with Grandpa was shortly after the assassinations of Dr. Martin Luther King and Robert Kennedy. He gave me a strong lecture on what it meant to be a man and stand up for what I believed in, no matter what the cost. My grandfather was an inspiring figure to me and became even more so after he died.

*If you tame me, then we shall need each other. To me, you will be unique in all the world. To you, I shall be unique in all the world.*
*Saint-Exupery*

## Evening Prayer 9:4

*Love does not cause suffering: what causes it is the sense of ownership, which is love's opposite.*
*Saint-Exupery*

**Dear God,** I ask for Your help. I have held a long-standing resentment against organized religion. I feel I was misled concerning my relationship with You and my relationship to myself. I need to be released from the anger I feel. I ask for Your patience as I develop a greater love of the historical Church. I want to feel union again with a community of people that worship You. It makes sense to me that if I turn my will and my life over to You, I should also come to worship You. I ask that as I grow in spirituality, You help me set aside my childish hurt and anger. I want to grow up. Amen.

*You can end love more easily than you can moderate it.*
*Seneca the Elder*

## Evening Reflection 9:4

*The course of true love never did run smooth.*
*Shakespeare*

I was in Brussels on a business trip. The meeting I attended finished three days earlier than scheduled. I decided to take the extra time and visit Ireland. I called my brother from London and got the name of a cousin in County Cork. When I arrived at Shannon Airport, how eerie and quiet everything seemed! I remembered reading about the Celtic twilight and knew I was a first-hand visitor to the misty place. I was amazed as I drove to see empty old buildings everywhere. I thought the Irish must have a phobia against tearing anything down.

I was to discover that the Irish and their history are inseparable. They have strong emotions about events that occurred a century ago. There is a timeless quality about the land.

I found my cousin and asked her to help me track my roots. I wanted to see the places where my forebears lived, died and were buried. On the last day of my trip, I asked my cousin to show me my family's ancient farmhouse in County Kerry. It was hard to find and harder to get to. We reached the area late in the afternoon. The sun had set and it was a roaring, windy night.

We trekked up a hill and knocked at the door of the nearest house. An old woman answered, and I introduced myself. She put her hands to her face and gasped, "You wouldn't be being Paddy's boy?" I replied, "No, ma'am, I think I would be being Paddy's grandboy." She threw her arms around me and gave me a warm hug. She hurried me in, sat me down by the open hearth, poured me a cup of tea, and proceeded to tell me all about my family. She spoke of events that had occurred 70 and 80 years ago as if they were yesterday. She told me about my great-grandfather and his father. I was filled with history.

I asked her where the old family homestead stood. She told me, "Walk down the lane a quarter mile and see for yourself." Down the road I went. I found an old rock house with no windows or chimneys. The British used to tax windows and chimneys. My people could not afford the tax so they did without. The entire family lived in this house, with the sheep and chickens. I chipped a piece of rock off the house and put it in my pocket. As I walked back to the cottage, I marvelled at my inadvertent luck, to get this opportunity to visit Ireland.

I sat with the old woman and asked her about herself. She told me of growing up a few miles away and how she thought at one point about going to America. I asked her why she hadn't.

To my amazement, she told me the same tale I had heard from grandfather. She had never gotten his letters. She never knew that my grandfather wanted her to come to America and marry him.

I told her the stories my grandfather had shared with me: the letters he had sent, the fact he did not hear from her, his last letter. I told her my grandfather had always loved her and nothing would have pleased him more than saying it to her face to face. He died before that could happen. She wept with me as we hugged. The wound that had not been closed for sixty years was at last healed.

God finally sent the amends that had been waiting all that time. She left me with this thought. "I have told you of the legacy your forebears left for you. You have given me the legacy your grandfather left for me. I wonder, dear boy, what legacy you will leave?"

*Love, whether sexual, parental, or fraternal, is essentially sacrificial, and prompts a man to give his life for his friends.*
*George Santayana*

## Morning Promise 9:1

*The greatest happiness you can have is knowing that you do not necessarily require happiness.*
*William Saroyan*

The promise of absolution is like getting a birthday card every day. I walk to my mailbox and find an envelope with my name on it. I open it and the card greets me with "Happy Birthday. You are another day older." Inside it reads, "I love you very much. You are accepted. Simply accept the fact. Signed, God." Every day of my life I get this card. If I live to be 80 years old I get it 29,200 times! Thank You, Lord, for loving and accepting me.

*It is one of the beautiful compensations of this life that no one can sincerely try to help another without helping himself.*
*Charles Dudley Warner*

## Morning Reflection 9:1

*The happiest is he who suffers the least pain; the most miserable, he who enjoys the least pleasure.*
*Rousseau*

The promise of absolution is not to help me reconstruct my broken world. The kind of sorrow I experienced before Step One was a hopeless display of self-pity and remorse. Absolution permanently lays to rest life-threatening bonds with the past. I move into the future as a free and loved human being. I cannot move into the future until I have taken Step Nine.

The promise of absolution is my declaration of citizenry in the world again. This time I am capable of being a good, compassionate citizen. Absolution allows me to finally get on with the business of living.

*A string of excited, fugitive, miscellaneous pleasures is not happiness; happiness resides in imaginative reflection and judgment, when the picture of one's life, or of human life, as it truly has been or is, satisfies the will, and is gladly accepted.*
*George Santayana*

## Morning Promise 9:2

*A peasant and a philosopher may be equally satisfied, but not equally happy. Happiness consists in the multiplicity of agreeable consciousness.*
*Samuel Johnson*

The promise of absolution follows my Ninth Step like day follows night. I have stuffed so many things from my life into shoeboxes and hidden them away, never to see the light of day: stealing my mother's car for a joyride, skipping school because I was "sick," the times my first girlfriend and I would sneak away together under the guise of "going to the library," the time I borrowed a term paper from Father Jack and turned it in as my own. All the accumulated boxes of stored away secrets are thrown away. The promise of the Ninth Step is that it has all been forgiven because it has all been taken in. My secrets make me sick; the Ninth Step gives me health.

*No matter how dull, or how mean, or how wise a man is, he feels that happiness is his indisputable right.*
*Helen Keller*

## Morning Reflection 9:2

*Often we can help each other most by leaving each other alone; at other times we need the handgrasp and the word of cheer.*
*Elbert Hubbard*

I had a friend named Frank. He had been in and out of AA for years. He had read all the material but could not stay sober. He worked the first three steps and that was all.

Frank was the kind of drinker who liked to go out and hoot and holler. If he wasn't able to get out, he would get on the phone. If he had a friend in Hong Kong, he would call Hong Kong and talk for hours. Frank was everyone's best friend. Alcohol didn't make him moody and morose; it livened him up.

A destitute old woman lived down the street from Frank. She had been alone for years and was crippled with arthritis. She had no friends or family. We all wondered how she got to the store to buy food. She was always watering or pruning a flower box full of pansies.

Time passed and the woman died. I went to her wake and saw Pete, a local grocery store owner, with Frank. When Frank moved away, I joined Pete, commenting that I hadn't realized he knew the lady. He replied he hadn't, but Frank did. "Really?" I said. "I didn't know that." Pete answered, "Sure. Every week Frank would come by the store and buy her a week's worth of groceries." The lady never knew who bought them; they just appeared on her porch each week. Frank was that kind of man. He was also an alcoholic.

*Happiness is a thing of gravity. It seeks for hearts of bronze, and carves itself there slowly; pleasure startles it away by tossing flowers to it. Joy's smile is much more close to tears than it is to laughter.*
*Victor Hugo*

## Morning Promise 9:3

*That thou art happy, owe to God; that thou continuest such, owe to thyself, that is, to thy obedience.*
*Milton*

As a young boy I feared confession. The idea of telling my sins to an anonymous priest would physically frighten me. Perhaps I suspected the prelate really knew who I was. As I grew older, it was not confession I feared; it was judgment. My sins seemed larger than life to me. I actually would go to confession and confess sins that I had not yet committed but planned to commit. I thought maybe if I died during the commission of one of these sins, my absolution would be retroactive from my last confession. Absolution was all tied up with judgment. Judgment was all tied up with damnation. I felt all tied up about both. In Step Nine, I discover that the judgment of God is mercy. I am required to account for my life so I can experience the full measure of God's love.

*We should consider every day lost on which we have not danced at least once. And we should call every truth false which was not accompanied by at least one laugh.*
*Nietzsche*

## Morning Reflection 9:3

*There are many roads to happiness, if the gods assent.*
*Pindar*

One day when Frank was drunk, he got in a car-driving mood. Off he went, headed for no particular destination. As he rounded a corner, he saw little Karen crossing the street, hauling a wagon with her four dolls in it. Frank was moving too fast to stop. He leaned on his horn to no avail. He hit Karen. She was caught on his bumper and dragged. Frank saw her in his rear-view mirror but did not stop. He fled the scene of his crime.

Little Karen was dead. The accident was reported as a hit and run. The funeral was a crushing experience for everyone. As the priest read the sermon, those four little dolls were perched on the altar rail looking down on the casket. You could almost see them crying.

I noticed Frank in the back pew. He was sobbing. I pulled him off after the service and asked if he wanted to talk. He said yes, very much. He told me about the accident, that he had been drinking and driving around, that he was the one who had struck Karen. He begged me to help him.

I checked Frank into a motel. I wrote down on a piece of paper the pages in the Big Book that I wanted him to read. It started with the Third Step prayer and continued through the promises. I told him to enter the motel room with pen and paper. I wanted him to do exactly as the book instructed. I told him that when he was ready to read me the account of his Fourth Step, I would be available. Approximately 16 hours later I got the call. I came back to the motel to hear his Fifth Step. After 5-1/2 hours, Frank was back on his knees reciting the Seventh Step prayer. I didn't understand what was happening to Frank, but I knew it was very deep. He stayed another 24 hours in the motel, working through his list of amends, calling people, writing people fervently. Finally, he asked for a ride. I got a cab. We rode to the police station and Frank turned himself in.

He was convicted of involuntary manslaughter. He is doing his time, making his amends. He may be in prison, but he is a free man. He has experienced absolution. Karen's parents have forgiven him. They even visit him in prison. He wrote me he is the secretary of his home group and is carrying the message to other inmates. He is going to school and will come out of prison with a degree. He included a picture of his cell. There on

Frank's shelf were the old lady's pansies, alive and well. And there on his cot were Karen's four dolls.

*A man's happiness - to do the things proper to man.*
*Marcus Aurelius*

## Morning Promise 9:4

*We have no more right to consume happiness without producing it than to consume wealth without producing it.*
*George Bernard Shaw*

The promise of absolution is a promise I have run from throughout my life. When I had opportunities to tell the truth, I often fabricated falsehoods. I was defending myself against the consequences of truth. That is a little like defending yourself against the consequences of winning the lottery. My life was marked by a search for perfection. My emotions froze in suspended animation. I saw correctness of behavior as the yardstick for judgment. Life became a battle to protect inches, not win miles. I was on guard at all moments to keep the discontinuity of life away from me. There is an adage that says "Shit happens." I covered myself with yards of insulation, thinking to protect myself. In Step Nine, I embrace absolution. My new life is fueled by my experiences. The indiscretions of the past become the fuel of the future.

*Happiness of any given life is to be measured, not by its joys and pleasures, but by the extent to which it has been free from suffering - from positive evil.*
*Schopenhauer*

## Morning Reflection 9:4

*How bitter a thing it is to look into happiness through another man's eyes!*
*Shakespeare*

After I do my Fifth Step I am given the assurance of forgiveness. In living my own forgiveness, I participate in absolution. Absolution occurs when I declare my accountability to life. I may have a lifetime of neglect and wasted efforts. I may have strewn my world with the wreckage of my actions. I may have hung my head in shame more than I have held it up in pride.

No matter what, if I embrace my Step work, I can be assured of two realities. First, I will have forgiveness before God. Second, I will be called to account for my actions before man. It is in these two spiritual exercises that I am given the promise of absolution. Faith is not something to be timid about. I can trust God and own up to my life, for I have the promise of absolution.

*It is God's giving if we laugh or weep.*
*Sophocles*

# STEP TEN

Continued to take personal inventory and when we were wrong promptly admitted it.

## Evening Prayers and Reflections for Discipline

## Morning Promises and Reflections of Devotion

## Evening Prayer 10:1

*We should render a service to a friend to bind him closer to us, and to an enemy in order to make a friend of him.*
*Cleobulus*

**O Bringer Of Seasons Faithfully Each Year,** I am happy to know more about the truth of life than I did before. These Steps have revealed so much. Last month I stood on a bridge that crossed a gully close to where I once lived. The trees were all stripped bare; fall and winter had made claim on all the foliage that dressed the trees during the summer. I thought, "If I were seeing this for the first time, there is no way I could believe there would be any possibility anything could grow on those bare limbs." Yet I know that by nature's miracle, spring will come, bringing new buds to blossom into foliage. The discipline of nature is that life follows death and death follows life, on and on. Am I any different? No. No different at all. Amen.

*Nothing is troublesome that we do willingly.*
*Thomas Jefferson*

## Evening Reflection 10:1

*The way to avoid evil is not by maiming our passions, but by compelling them to yield their vigor to our moral nature.*
*Henry Ward Beecher*

When I am conscious of having fun, I experience everything more intensely. I am consumed with a "life wish." I am keeping an open channel to my Higher Power. Discipline creates the environment for me to be continually free.

The fable of the Three Little Pigs gives me some insight into this concept. The three pigs all had approximately the same backgrounds. They all knew basically the kind of world in which they lived and what dangers might await them. One was unconscious, the second was slightly conscious, and the third was wide awake.

The unconscious pig exercised no discipline. When he built his house, he allowed himself to forget about his enemy, the wolf. When the wolf made his move, it was curtains for pig one's house of straw.

Pig two had some consciousness about his life, but his ego was still too big. He figured he could outsmart the wolf. He calculated wrong. He lost and down came his house.

The third pig did not waste time trying to outsmart the wolf. He understood the power of his enemy and respected it. He had discipline. When he built his house he was conscious of what the wolf could do. So when the wolf tried to blow his house down, the pig was ready.

I always seem to fall somewhere in between. I continue to let my ego creep into my life and distort my consciousness. I am continually having to take personal inventory. I build my house too weak for prevailing conditions and promptly try to make the house suitable to live in.

I find I can copy things that work for other people and make them my own. I watch what I let into my mind and heart. I learn to sense who will keep me conscious and who will not. I discriminate. I take note of what I read, what T.V. and movies I watch. I try to take care of my health. I exercise, not simply to look good, but because it is part of being conscious. I take careful note of my space, making sure it communicates the right things to me. I take note of how I look. I am engaging in a love affair with myself. I treat myself as someone I love.

There are not many days I can maintain 100% consciousness. That means I will sometimes act like the dumb little pig. Not to worry - forgiveness abounds, as long as I immediately act on my mistakes and ask forgiveness for them.

*He that doth a good turn looketh for a good turn.*
*Thomas Fuller*

## Evening Prayer 10:2

*A man who is master of himself can end a sorrow as easily as he can invent a pleasure.*
*Oscar Wilde*

**O Patient Friend,** I have the attention span of a two-year-old. I seem to be distracted by every passing person. The discipline to remain keenly focused on Your will for me escapes me more often than not. I continually play the "what if" game: what if I meet her, what if I get this job, what if I win the lottery, what if I get cancer, what if they don't like me? On and on. Sometimes I give these games weighty importance in my life. They lay claim on all my plans. They compete with the decision I made in Step Three. They never make the anticipated payoff. Why do I let the game go on? Perhaps today I will spend one less minute so engaged. If so, I will say progress. Amen.

*Time brings all things to pass.*
*Aeschylus*

## Evening Reflection 10:2

*Time ripens all things. No man's born wise.*
*Cervantes*

Mother Theresa had a revelation on the train from Bombay to Calcutta. She felt an overpowering outpouring of divine light that filled her with love. Was Mother Theresa's experience any different than my own revelatory encounter with a Higher Power? It doesn't matter. What matters is the revelation.

God works on divine time. His time is not my time. I wonder why I spent so many years beaten by my addiction. Why did I have to lose so much and hurt so badly before I found my way into the Twelve Steps? Questioning God's will is useless. The experience speaks for itself. No amount of self-guessing will change the fact that my appointed hour came exactly when it was scheduled.

*Time is the only true purgatory.*
*Samuel Butler*

## Evening Prayer 10:3

*It is not the whip that makes men, but the lure of things that are worthy to be loved.*
*Woodrow Wilson*

**O Benevolent Freedom Giver,** I understand my limits as never before, and I do not feel bound by them. There is no harsh condemnation from my

God. The God of my youth was a stern judge. I felt fear whenever Your name was mentioned. Hopelessness characterized my attitude toward You. My sins mounted. I thought if I continued to believe in You as I had been taught, my soul would be condemned for all eternity. I chose to believe in nothing instead. After years in the temporal hell I had created with alcohol, an entirely different God was revealed to me, a God of light, love, direction. The discipline imposed in following this Higher Power brought peace of mind. The judgment of this God on my life is redemption. Amen.

*Life is always a discipline, for the lower animals as well as for men; it is so dangerous that only by submitting to some sort of discipline can we become equipped to live in any true sense at all.*
*Havelock Ellis*

## Evening Reflection 10:3

*Man who man would be, must rule the empire of himself.*
*Shelley*

The first time I realized I could not dictate the outcome of life was the day my grandmother died. I was eleven. I had never been particularly close to my grandmother, but I did know her as flesh and blood, alive. Her body in the funeral home was like plastic. The cold stark reality of death made my skin crawl. When my father wailed in sorrow, when my grandfather threw himself on her casket, when all the adults sobbed in sadness, my theories about angels, heaven and eternal peace fell apart. How could all these people, who went to church and held the same beliefs I did, find no comfort in the "now she is in heaven" story? It did not make sense to me.

We went to the cemetery for the graveside service. The casket sat on green carpet under an awning. Next to the casket was a big mound covered by another green carpet.

A man in a dirty jumpsuit stood a few yards off. I walked over to him and asked him what he did. He told me when the ceremony was over, he would lower the casket into the hold and fill it with the dirt covered up by the green carpet. Then he would take the awning down and roll the cut grass over the filled-up hole. When he finished that report, I exhaled a long breath. Dying was taking on a much uglier look.

I asked him what happened after the casket was under the earth. I was hoping to hear it would miraculously disappear into the realm of heaven. He said caskets were constructed to disintegrate over time, and the body decayed along with the casket. Eventually the earth, the body and the casket became one.

Death had never been explained to me quite like that. The man in the dirty jumpsuit was the person who was really going to put my grandmother into her final resting place, not some winged angel. It all seemed a lie, the phony green carpet covering the real dirt that would be thrown into the hole after the biodegradable casket was put in its last resting place.

After Grandma's funeral, I became depressed, isolated and reclusive. I quit going to school. I searched for places to hide: closets, under beds and up in trees. Each morning my parents had to search for me. If reality was going to get me, I would go down fighting. Finally, my parents quit forcing me to go to school. My books came home. I studied in the morning and saw a psychiatrist in the afternoon. I discovered that if I spoke of ending it all and joining my grandma, the doctor would order pills for me that made me feel happy. It all seemed so simple. I would demand to be left alone, insist that if I was not, I would kill myself, and wait for the adults in my life to back down. I would not live on life's terms *if I had a choice*. I languished in my make-believe world for four months after the funeral. Finally an old Irish priest told my father he ought to try a different approach to my disobedience. He should beat me.

*What it lies in our power to do, it lies in our power not to do.*
*Aristotle*

## Evening Prayer 10:4

*We can't reach old age by another man's road.*
*Mark Twain*

**O Final Mentor,** I have found freedom in a strange place, squarely in the midst of obedience. When I was young, I hated the discipline and regimentation of school. The teachers seemed like totally unsympathetic taskmasters. One day I packed myself a lunch and ran away from home. I wasn't sure where to go, but I knew I had to head in the opposite direction of school. Soon I had finished my lunch and become quite lost. When I realized I did not know the way home, I grew frightened. The more frightened I felt, the less I hated school. I made all the pledges and promises that if I found my way home, I would never hate school again. Finally I reached the crest of a hill and saw something I recognized -- the school. From that day on, that brick schoolhouse looked a lot less like prison and a lot more like home. Amen.

*The tissue of Life to be we weave with colors all our own, and in the field of Destiny we reap as we have sown.*
*John Greenleaf Whittier*

## Evening Reflection 10:4

*We are all, it seems, saving ourselves for the Senior Prom. But many of us forget that somewhere along the way we must learn to dance.*
*Alan Harrington*

The idea of discipline in contemporary life seems almost foreign. The hangover from the sixties has most people still running from the thought of personal discipline. All who have experienced the ravages of addiction know only too well the futility of will power. From my earliest memories I was taught the virtues of personal restraint, will power, and self-control. I was taught about a God who helped those who helped themselves. Discipline was the armed forces. It was fascist Germany. It was infringement on personal liberty.

It is hard to pray for something I need but don't want. Men and women who are spiritual are disciplined. People who exercise discipline in their lives do not find that discipline in their minds or their wills. Spiritual discipline flows as naturally from the Tenth Step as courage flows from the Fifth, humility from the Seventh, or charity from the Eighth. Discipline finds its power source in spiritual vitality, which the Step work I do creates. I have turned away from a life lived on my own personal energy. I no longer feed on myself. Alcohol, drugs, food or other people are no longer consumed as fuel for my personal power. My new power source is God. I get my batteries charged from a Power greater than me, and that Power is unlimited. How can I be tired if I am not being propelled by my own resources?

To most of us, discipline is like a harness around the neck of a wild stallion. I think I am disciplined when I break the wild horse within me.

What breaks is more often my own creativity, my enthusiasm for life, my motivation. The essence of my personality becomes a rule book of dos and don'ts. No wonder I steer clear of the concept of discipline. I would rather be beaten than discipline myself. It is sometimes surprising how much discipline I exercise in my efforts not to be disciplined.

Step Ten is prompt daily admissions of truth. It is staying on top of my spiritual condition. Step Ten is preventative medicine. My prayer for discipline is foremost a prayer for consciousness. Why is this so? First, I must realize that discipline is not blind obedience, nor is it mindless adherence to habit patterns. This is what got me into trouble in the first place. I thought I was undisciplined when I played into my addictions. On the contrary, it took great personal resolve to stay on my deadly course. The discipline I pray for in Step Ten is the spiritual kind. It comes from being conscious, like an Indian with his ear to the earth, sensing the movements of animals. Radar O'Reilly of "Mash" fame always knew when the choppers were on their way. It is consciousness of the kind animals have when they sense a change in weather patterns. Discipline is being tuned into intuition.

Once again, my old nemesis, the mind, is my greatest foe. I must put the mind in its proper place. It must be taught that it does not have absolute knowledge of good and evil. The mind lusts after itself and manifests its perversion in rationalizations. When I exercise consciousness in my life, I am not rationalizing. The key to becoming a spiritual person is learning how to shut my mind down so that I can tune into a deeper wellspring of sensitivity. Consciousness is knowing when I have no idea how I know. It is sensing something evil when I have nothing on which to base my opinion. It is knowing something is good for me when I don't know why it is good. Consciousness bypasses reason to get at the truth. Discipline comes from the source within me that is the most wildly creative force imaginable. Discipline comes from the wild horse, not the harness.

*For all your days prepare, and meet them all alike: when you are the anvil, bear - when you are the hammer, strike.*
*Edwin Markham*

# Morning Promise 10:1

*You will fetter my leg, but not Zeus himself can get the better of my free will.*
*Epictetus*

The promise of devotion is like finding in myself the love of a mother for her baby. My recovery becomes a precious, vulnerable young life. It requires my most tender behavior. There are days I am fragile and frail. I am constantly reminded to go easy on myself, take it step by step, live and let live, easy does it. As I live by these admonitions I find myself devoted to my recovery and loving myself because of what is being revealed about me. The baby I have always been is finally getting the nurture for which it always begged, yet seldom received. Devotion to myself is not a new form of egotism or conceit. Devotion to myself is my way of loving, honoring and obeying my covenant to myself. God surely stands with me individually, just as God stands with all people. The promise of devotion binds me to myself with the loving commitment to think good about myself, to do good to myself, and to forever be good to myself.

*Some minds seem almost to create themselves, springing up under every disadvantage and working their solitary but irresistible way through a thousand obstacles.*
*Washington Irving*

# Morning Reflection 10:1

*In the history of the individual is always an account of his condition, and he knows himself to be a party to his present estate.*
*Emerson*

Finally after a lifetime of searching for life's most cherished experience, I find this elusive devotion in the nitty gritty business of being disciplined. I become a transmitter of consciousness. My work with Twelve Step spirituality transforms the categories of love and devotion in my life. Devotion becomes something that moves through me as I daily discover God's will for me. As I keep myself tuned into God's will, I find myself being a lover. I am no longer struggling to find this or that; I am no longer primarily concerned for my own love. I have become rooted in love and no longer need to search for that which I have already become.

The spiritual promise is for true devotion. As the Steps become my way of life, a spiritual path, they completely transform my perspective on devotion. It bears no resemblance to a dime store romance novel. It more resembles the discovery of my true vocation in life.

The world stands in awe of Mother Theresa, the nun who started the Order of Sisters that cares for the sick and dying in Calcutta, India. She has attracted such attention with her work that she was awarded the Nobel Peace Prize in 1985.

Why mention Mother Theresa in the context of the Tenth Step Promise? I am not suggesting that by virtue of doing a Tenth Step I set myself up for sainthood. I must dispel from my mind the old images of saints, nuns and other people of the cloth. Mother Theresa's story has practical significance for people who seek spirituality. She was, in her early years, indistinguishable from any other nun in her order. She was not born with great virtue and holiness. She was a girl from a good home who felt a calling to become a Roman Catholic Sister. Most of us understand that the simple fact of becoming religious does not make one a better person than someone who chooses, say, to be a fisherman. It is not the exterior vocation that makes a difference; it is the interior spirituality. Then how was it that this ordinary nun became such an extraordinary example of devotion? Many people assume she went to Calcutta, saw the starving, the dying, the millions of neglected souls and decided she would spend the rest of her life caring for these people. They believe she simply saw a human need and became willing to fill that need.

This would be a plausible story, but the fact is it didn't happen that way at all. Mother Theresa didn't start her order of nuns until she was middle aged. She had been among the poor on many occasions and never felt called to work with them. The calling she received had nothing to do with the poor, hungry, dying people of Calcutta. It had to do with a spiritual experience so powerful she became totally devoted to its message.

*I have discovered that we may be in some degree whatever character we choose. Besides, practice forms a man to anything.*
*James Boswell*

## Morning Promise 10:2

*A bad beginning makes a bad ending.*
*Euripides*

The promise of devotion reminds me of my grandfather's relationship to Ireland. My grandfather immigrated when he was a young man. He left in a time of turmoil. The country was on the verge of revolution. He was deeply in love with the vision and spirit of those times. He was devoted to what he saw as Ireland's future. No sacrifice was too great to usher in the new day. He was forced to leave his beloved country. The farm could not support the whole family. He left; Ireland had its revolution. It made no difference what happened after the uprising, my grandfather remained devoted to the cause. It made no difference what he did in America. In his mind and heart he remained an Irishman, fighting for Ireland's freedom and its future. His devotion was not to a specific set of goals but to a general set of principles. My grandfather lived in a world where principles mattered, and poetry books were as important as engineering books. I don't know if Grandpa ever got the facts straight. His stories were often fictional. His truth, though, was always unmistakable: devotion to a cause is the most important, vital force a man or woman will ever know. Grandpa always greeted me in the same way: "How are you, lad, and where do you stand?" Always, where do you stand? To what are you devoted?

*A mighty flame followeth a tiny spark.*
*Dante*

## Morning Reflection 10:2

*The consequences of our actions take hold of us quite indifferent to our claim that meanwhile we have "improved."*
*Nietzsche*

When I continue to take personal inventory, I keep my flame lit, my eyes focused, my mind open, my heart burning. My personal inventory lets me remember it is God I am loving, and in loving God I have abundant fulfillment. When I am distracted by my own pain, when I find old patterns still haunting me, I choose not to give them power over me. I immediately take steps to admit I made a mistake. I never have to go back to the places I travelled before I started my Twelve Step program. The inventory shows me a way of staying current with the truth.

The promise of love in my Tenth Step is a tender reminder that I have light in my life, one that will never go out if I clean my wick daily. When I lay my head down to sleep, I can rest assured that I will wake up to light. I can close my eyes to the prayer I learned as a child and know finally what those words meant: "Now I lay me down to sleep, I pray the Lord my soul to keep. If I die before I wake, I pray the Lord my soul to take." Thank you, Higher Power.

*How great a matter a little fire kindleth!*
*Bible*

## Morning Promise 10:3

*Both in thought and in feeling, even though time be real, to realize the unimportance of time is the gate of wisdom.*
*Bertrand Russell*

The promise of devotion is exciting. After years of wondering what in life is important, it is like a light going on. My life has seen the collapse of many sacred cows. I was born into an age of rebellion and war. The battles I fought inevitably saw institutions collapse: education, marriages, professions, friendships, religions. Nothing was too sacred or too good that it could not be subjected to the cynical judgment that this was a new age and nothing should look as it once did. In my lifetime I've seen broken heroes, shattered institutions and convoluted values. The illuminating promise of Step Ten is that my life can be filled with such value that I can be fulfilled. Whether it be a relationship, a marriage, a profession, a church, I know that with my devotion all these can become profoundly important to me. Such devotion shines bright on the miracle of my recovery.

*Time makes more converts than reason.*
*Thomas Paine*

## Morning Reflection 10:3

*Time is a kindly God.*
*Sophocles*

A second lesson I can learn from Mother Theresa is that footwork must occur after I have had my revelation. The matter of staying conscious is a day to day decision. When Mother Theresa landed in Calcutta, she saw things differently. She saw God in everything and everyone. She had only one burning desire, to love God. She cultivated this desire. She surrounded herself with people who wanted to capture a piece of her vision. She immediately took steps to remind herself that loving her Higher Power was her only concern. She found that this love was best expressed working among the poor, the destitute and the dying. The fact that she saw the face of God in the faces of dying people is only more dramatic than seeing the face of God in a classroom. The revelation is the same. When I saw the Sister caring for the dying beggar in Bombay, my response was to run away. I did not see God's face on that dying man. When I looked at that man I saw my own death.

When I am visited by my Higher Power and acknowledge the presence of God in my life, I remain the same. If I take my acknowledgement and decide to turn my will and my life over to God, then I too will see His face in all my encounters. I too will want to nurture that experience. I must wait for God to act in my life. Nothing good can happen for me until God happens first.

*God Himself chasteneth not with a rod but with time.*
*Baltasar Gracian*

## Morning Promise 10:4

*Quite often good things have hurtful consequences. There are instances of men who have been ruined by their money or killed by their courage.*
*Aristotle*

The promise of devotion has to do with keeping promises. I have pledged oaths, entered into covenants, said binding words, affixed my name to agreements I knew I would not keep. It isn't that I didn't intend to keep my word and honor my obligations, it is that I was powerless over the behavior that led me to disavow my commitments. The promise of devotion comes to me as the purity of heart to live my life one day at a time. As I work my program and develop my conscious contact with God each day, I find the devotion spilling over into my other daily commitments. As a child, I loved watching Westerns on T.V. Whether it was The Lone Ranger, Hopalong Cassidy, Rin Tin Tin, Bonanza, The Rifleman, Sugarfoot, Cheyenne, Wyatt Earp, the heroes always had honor. They always stood against the forces of evil, people who had no honor. As a child, I saw in uncomplicated terms the fruits of honor. Now as a promise earned through daily due diligence, I am given doses of devotion. I become a person of honor, a hero in my own life.

*Does not every true man feel that he is himself made higher by doing reverence to what is really above him?*
*Thomas Carlyle*

## Morning Reflection 10:4

*Happiness is like a sunbeam, which the least shadow intercepts.*
*Chinese Proverb*

When I was ten, I learned about life's shortcut to experience: lying. I would make up answers to questions the teacher would ask about my family. My mother's maiden name was McCoy. I would tell great stories about how my mother's family was truly the "real McCoy," and how she as a little girl fought with the real "Hatfield family." Since at the time there was a television show titled the "Real McCoys," I was borrowing on that fame to become famous myself. My dad was a salesman for a plastics company. Instead of admitting this, I would say he owned the company and had started the entire plastics business in the Northwest.

I had opinions about which I knew absolutely nothing. I elevated myself to make myself bigger, smarter, better looking than the next person. I hated to compete in any sporting event, not because I was a poor athlete, but because the chance of losing was more than I could bear. If you played baseball, you could miss a groundball, you could strike out. The truth could not be shaded. Any event whose outcome was outside my control became an event to shy away from. Head to head competition of any kind was a painful and chilling experience.

*Half of the results of a good intention are evil; half the results of an evil intention are good.*
*Mark Twain*

# STEP ELEVEN

Sought through prayer and meditation to improve our conscious contact with God *as we understood Him*, praying only for knowledge of His will for us and the power to carry that out.

## Evening Prayers and Reflections for Faithfulness

## Morning Promises and Reflections of Vocation

## Evening Prayer 11:1

*One cannot be strong with love. For love is not an irrelevant emotion; it is the blood of life, the power of reunion of the separated.*
*Paul Tillich*

**O Great Provider Of Miracles,** why is it things happen just at the moment they should? Am I to assume that You actually know what You are doing and care about why You are doing it? What comes to me as an appearance is to You standard operating procedure. I have come to know You as a loving Power Who intimately and personally cares about my well-being. This is not to say everything I have wanted for myself has been granted me. On the contrary, much of what I have wanted has not happened. Yet I have to admit that what has been given me, even against my will, has been exactly right for me. What can I assume other than that You know what is good for me? I ask only that I trust Your will as it is revealed to me on a daily basis. My prayer for faithfulness is to embrace that which will never fail me. Amen.

*If so many hearts, so many kinds of love.*
*Leo Tolstoy*

## Evening Reflection 11:1

*Love is like those shabby hotels in which all the luxury is in the lobby.*
*Paul Jian Toulet*

There is an intimacy within the person in recovery that produces intense feelings. The proven compatibility between an individual and a Higher Power creates deep spiritual affection. I am a baby held tenderly to the bosom of life. At the same time I guard my spiritual connection like a mother lion guards her den. I experience both sides of the birthing equation. I am both mother and child. Each new day delivers so much new growth. In my pregnancy I want to watch how I live so I don't jeopardize what is being born within me.

The full dimensions of 12 Step recovery create an abundant spirituality. I have come to know a life unlike anything I have ever known. In the past, I attempted to change the world so it would be possible for me to live in it. Now I have changed myself so I can live in the world. The prayer I make as I enter Step Eleven is for faithfulness and fidelity. Prayer and meditation let me focus on the love in my life. I cannot help but feel a personal relationship with God. He is no longer an abstract, bearded, vengeful Father who punishes me for every misstep. That tyrant has been replaced by a benevolent Power Who has caring qualities unmatched in their feminine tenderness and masculine strength. My words are heard and unconditionally accepted. I no longer fear to bring my deepest longings to my Higher Power. I rely on the admonishment, "Let Go and Let God." Before, I thought I could only bring God my completed accomplishments, like a quarterly report card. In those days, my visits with Him were few and far between. Now I can bring to Him daily anything and everything I collect. My Eleventh Step agenda is always full.

*The absolute value of love makes life worthwhile, and so makes Man's strange and difficult situation acceptable. Love cannot save life from death; but it can fulfill life's purpose.*
*Arnold J. Toynbee*

## Evening Prayer 11:2

*Love is an act of endless forgiveness, a tender look which becomes a habit.*
*Peter Ustinov*

**O Most Loyal One,** I am reminded of my friend Bruce. Bruce had a horse he raised from the colt's birth. He liked to say that the horse really raised him. Fletch was most faithful to Bruce; Bruce in turn was devoted to Fletch. Bruce spent most of his time with Fletch. Neighbors thought something was wrong with Bruce, that he was antisocial. Bruce was experiencing a unique relationship. One day Bruce was out with Fletch and it began to snow. As he turned to begin the trek home, his head hit a low branch and he was knocked down. Bruce was out cold, and Fletch knew there was trouble. The horse lay down beside Bruce and kept him warm through the night. As day broke and Bruce's condition seemed to worsen, Fletch covered Bruce with a warm blanket of earth and left for home. He stood in front of the house until Bruce's brother Bill came out. Bill, realizing something was wrong, mounted the horse. Fletch took him back to Bruce. Bruce lived to tell about his encounter with faithfulness. It does not matter if Fletch was a horse, a rabbit, or governor of the state. Faithfulness looks like care, smells like care, and loves like care. Fletch was faithful to Bruce. Amen.

*Love has various lodgings; the same word does not always signify the same thing.*
*Voltaire*

## Evening Reflection 11:2

*By each let this be heard, some do it with a bitter look, some with a flattering word. The coward does it with a kiss, the brave man with a sword!*
*Oscar Wilde*

Faithfulness to God means loving only one God, serving only the Highest of Higher Powers. I have found the Master of my Universe. In Step Eleven I decide to look no further. I no longer God-hop in hopes of finding a God that I can control, a God that tells me it is O.K. to eat forbidden fruit. The prayer of faithfulness to God delivers me once again to my Third Step. I recall how I have pledged my will and my life to the care of God. I recall how in subsequent Steps I have learned the full range of God's power. I remember the Sixth Step prayer with earnestness:

"God, I offer myself to Thee - to build with me and to do with me as Thou wilt. Relieve me of the bondage of self, that I may better do Thy will. Take away my difficulties, that victory over me may bear witness to Thou I would help of Thy Power, Thy Love, and Thy Way of Life. May I do Thy will always." *Alcoholics Anonymous,* p. 76.

These words ring. I ask for the relationship always. The prayer I utter in the Eleventh Step is delivered by a person who now lives faithfully one day at a time. I have seen a miracle in my own life and have come to believe in that miracle. I turn over a half-measured will and have it given back to me as a strong and powerful resolve. I learn to live this miracle one day at a time. I make no assumptions about tomorrow. I live the miracle in the present time. The Eleventh Step is about tending to that miracle. I seek to listen to what is being asked of me. The will of God is discovered on a daily basis. This requires mechanisms for listening and discovering. Step Eleven is a mechanism for discerning God's will for me. Each day as I pray and meditate I feel the new surge of power I need to carry out that will.

*Love is an energy which exists of itself. It is its own value.*
*Thornton Wilder*

## Evening Prayer 11:3

*There is no fear in love; but perfect love casteth out fear.*
*Bible*

**O Father God,** why is it, when I have betrayed you on countless occasions, You remain faithful to me? How can You love a person who has continually turned his back on You? I assumed that the price I would pay for abandoning You would be eternal damnation. The truth is You loved me all along. You have patiently waited for me to notice Your love. The guilt I have borne around my neck like an albatross has been a tragic mistake. The God I have come to know has actually loved me all along. Your forgiveness is unlimited. You ask me to be faithful to that which loves me without question throughout time. The question seems almost foolish. Yet it is precisely the prayer that I make daily, a prayer for faithfulness to You. Amen.

*To fall in love is to create a religion that has a fallible god.*
*Jorge Luis Borges*

## Evening Reflection 11:3

*When you love someone all your saved-up wishes start coming out.*
*Elizabeth Bowen*

It is during my prayer and meditation moments I am most often tempted. My prayer for faithfulness at these times is that I listen only to God. The days of recovery are wonderful days. I feel great, I look better, and all aspects of my life are better. My program has turned white knuckle sobriety into full blown spiritual recovery. I accomplish things that in earlier days would have been impossible. I attend meetings and hear stories that amaze me. Then on a later occasion I speak at a meeting and afterward hear the plaudits of individuals who are grateful for my words. People begin to sense in me a quality they want.

These are the times I want to take serious care about my Step

Eleven. Now is the time I want to redouble my efforts to remain faithful to my Higher Power, because when things appear to be going well I hear the voices that tell me I did it on my own. Perhaps it comes in the form of a special new relationship. I have met the dream of my dreams, the perfect person. My tendency is to project the quality of a Higher Power on that person. I invest inordinate amounts of time, energy and spiritual resource in this special person. I think I am being normal, as if normality were ever a criteria for proper behavior. When I contemplate, meditate or pray, I drift off into fanciful daydreams about my love. I begin to lose touch with my Higher Power. Slowly I turn away from my friends in the program. They remind me of my disease. I say I want to put it all behind me so I can carry on with a "normal" life. All these voices sound so right. They are filled with bits and pieces of the truth.

They are actually chips at my spiritual foundation. I have begun a slow process of chipping away at my sobriety. After a while I am no longer living in conscious contact with a Higher Power. I have eaten of the fruit, and that fruit came to me in the form of another human being. These diversions can lead me right back into my addiction. Anyone who has ever touched the hand of God in life will know that no human touch is capable of giving as much. When I am unfaithful to my Higher Power, it is hard to find a way back. My ego becomes a force once again. Rather than walking with God, I wage war with God. Humiliation and embarrassment keep me outside the fold for months, sometimes years. I feel shamed, and I start digging new levels of despair and misery for myself.

Many never return. They die with their addiction. This story is told on countless occasions. The ending never varies - I lose conscious contact with my Higher Power and I lose contact with my one tool to keep my affliction from swallowing me. No amount of wishing this fact away will change it. I am in serious trouble when I rely on my own devices.

*The wish to lead out one's lover must be a tribal feeling; the wish to be seen as loved is part of one's self-respect.*
*Elizabeth Bowen*

# Evening Prayer 11:4

---

*Eternal Love doth keep in his complacent arms, the earth, the air, the deep.*
*William Cullen Bryant*

**O Beloved Lord**, there was a time when faithfulness to one's wife was the rule for marriage. It was not a struggle because there was really no option. Throughout history, fidelity in marriage was a cornerstone moral precept. This form of faithfulness was the glue which held whole societies together. The symbol was quite clear - the intimate bond between a man and woman was sacred. The sexual act was a clear symbol of God's presence in the relationship between a married couple. To abrogate this bond was to violate God. Over time I became confused about the symbol of marital faithfulness. Now I pray for faithfulness. I pray to be bound to Thee in everything I do. I pray that my marriage to this Power never be shattered by violating my decision. I bind myself to Thee because to be bound to You is to be bound to that which has unlimited forgiveness for a soul who wanders. You know me for who I am and what I am. It is Your knowledge of me that allows me to be faithful to You, that I may come to know You too. Amen.

*Love dies only when growth stops.*
*Pearl S. Buck*

## Evening Reflection 11:4

*To love a thing means wanting it to live.*
*Confucius*

The Step Eleven prayer for faithfulness clearly places me in the proper posture to receive the will of God and carry it out. When I pray and meditate as a faithful son, I hear only what God intends for me. The other cries that seek to divert my attention and disrupt me from my primary relationship are muffled. I must remember that each day I feel better, I must become increasingly more vigilant. Prayer and meditation are powerful forces. They, in themselves, can change the world. I must use this force constructively. Faithful service to God's will is the highest purpose, and my special calling.

*Friendship often ends in love; but love in friendship - never.*
*Charles Caleb Colton*

## Morning Promise 11:1

*When a man prays, do you know what he's doing? What? He's saying to himself: "Keep calm, everything's all right; it's all right."*
*Ugo Betti*

The promise of vocation is not like finding a profession. Vocation is not about being a teacher, a carpenter, or an engineer. Vocation is about my identity, about the fundamental purpose for which I have been placed on this earth. Vocation is the result of my faithfulness to my Higher Power. Vocation for most of us does not mean living in a monastery or convent. Spirituality is not necessarily found in those places; nor, for that matter, is vocation. A vocation is about my relationship with a Higher Power. When that relationship is real it causes me to act in a certain way. It permeates all my activities, whether I am changing diapers, changing tires or changing laws. My vocation reveals just how I express God's will in specific situations. The promise of vocation is that in deciding to know the will of God, I will also live the will of God.

*A prayer may chance to rise From one whose heart lives in the grace of God. A prayer from any other is unheeded.*
*Dante*

## Morning Reflection 11:1

*Prayer is the contemplation of the facts of life from the highest point of view.*
*Emerson*

The Garden of Gethsemane was for me the most powerful story in the New Testament. Jesus went with several of his disciples into a grove of olive trees to pray and meditate. He was there to sort out the will of God. He knew, from a lifetime of living in conscious contact with God, that during meditation and prayer He discovered God's will and received the power to carry it out. Jesus worked a program with shocking clarity and consistency.

This particular night, He was meditating on His impending death. Jesus, like the rest of us, knew that He would some day die. He also knew that He would be working His steps until the day He died. Jesus was on a spiritual path and was ever faithful to that path. He knew death was just around the corner. He struggled mightily with fear. He knew about the temptations that often come with the Eleventh Step. He asked His disciples to sit with Him. He wanted His colleagues close. This night was to be special. When Jesus went back to His friends, he found them sleeping. His disappointment was keen.

He was alone with the Higher Power He called Father. He began to pray out loud, begging for something other than the death He knew was facing Him. His trust was tested beyond any other time in His life.

*Prayer should be the key of the day and the lock of the night.*
*Thomas Fuller*

## Morning Promise 11:2

*Who rises from prayer a better man, his prayer is answered.*
*George Meredith*

The promise of vocation is an end to the incessant search for meaning in what I do. I remember my first interest in life was being an astronomer. That was before I found out how much math they had to know. Then for a time my dream was to be a lawyer. My desire was to carve out a role for myself in society. What I did would define who I was. My role would then dictate how people would treat me. What I did would define where I lived and with whom I lived. I could take charge and control the outcome of my life if I chose the right vocation. The promise of vocation was my deliverance from my life. The promise of Step Eleven is the opposite of what I was brought up to believe. The promise of Step Eleven is the promise of my vocation to be delivered through the will of Almighty God.

*My words fly up, my thoughts remain below. Words without thoughts never to heaven go.*
*Shakespeare*

## Morning Reflection 11:2

*Pray to God but continue to row to the shore.*
*Russian Proverb*

In the Garden of Gethsemane Jesus continued to wrestle with the Eleventh Step. Once again He walked back to get strength from His disciples. Once again He found them sleeping. He remembered the time spent in the desert, the forty days of intense meditation and prayer, the temptations. Jesus knew about voices. He saw three visions during his time in the desert. Each vision had features that looked inviting. Each vision had features of the truth. As He looked at His sleeping disciples, He accepted the fact that Step Eleven is solitary. When God speaks His will it is always an intensely personal experience. Jesus knew that now more than ever He needed a clear channel. He remembered it took all His spiritual strength to resist the temptations in the desert. Now His life was on the line. He must be sure. There was no room for half-measured truth. The next few hours must be all about living God's will.

The message was clear. He was to speak only the truth. He was to walk directly into the midst of His accusers. He was to be absolutely faithful to His program. He was then to accept the judgment of the world on His life. He was then to freely participate in the walk to Calvary to witness His own death. He was to carry with Him the instrument that would kill Him. He was to hold no resentment for anyone who participated in putting Him to death. Up to the last moment of His life He was to carry the message.

So it was. Jesus stood before His accusers and varied not one iota from His program. When His words produced a tempest of protest He stood and argued only for the truth, not to save His own life. When His steadfast stance caused Him to be sentenced to death, He took that verdict as a free man. He picked up His cross and walked as best He could to the spot He was to be killed. He mounted the cross forgiving those that were sent to kill Him. His program did not vary as the world watched him writhing in agony. The reports of His passing indicate that He carried the message up until the very last moments of His life. He shared with the man being crucified next to Him His Third Step and let the man know it would work for him too. Jesus "passed it on" right up until the end. He died letting go: "It is finished." The story of faithfulness is captured in the story of the last few hours in the life of Jesus.

*Today any successful and competent businessman will employ the latest and best-tested methods in production, distribution, and administration, and many are discovering that one of the greatest of all efficiency methods is prayer power.*
*Norman Vincent Peale*

## Morning Promise 11:3

*A great obstacle to happiness is to anticipate too great a happiness.*
*Fontenelle*

The promise of vocation was driven home to me one day when I visited a county hospital. A young man named Danny was brought in with a broken leg. He had been stricken with spinal meningitis when he was eight months old. His head was hydrocephalic. His body was only two feet in length. He was blind and deaf. Danny's mother and father had deserted him. He was alone with his condition, institutionalized in a state hospital. Danny's head had never lifted from his pillow. He had never seen his own image. He had never heard his own voice. He could not swallow food. His nourishment was pumped through a tube into his stomach. As I stood next to Danny, I saw he was crying. Somewhere inside his world he felt anguish. He was alone with only God to comfort him. I thought long about this encounter. How am I really any different from Danny? Vocation is the singular manifestation of a person's relationship with God. All Danny could do to manifest his obedience to the will of God was to cry. My options are more varied, perhaps, but my obedience can be no more complete than Danny's. The promise is fulfilled in such a vocation.

*He is happy that knoweth not himself to be otherwise.*
*Thomas Fuller*

## Morning Reflection 11:3

*Human felicity is produced not so much by great pieces of good fortune that seldom happen as by little advantages that occur every day.*
*Benjamin Franklin*

Step Eleven gives me the opportunity to learn God's will for me. When I am not doing the will of God I am not happy; I am not living in fulfillment. There is always something missing. The question for me is always, "How do I know what I am supposed to do?" How do I ferret out from all the clatter what is for me and what is not?

I do this through prayer and meditation. I must create the daily opportunity to be alone with my Higher Power and allow the knowledge of God's will to appear. Step Eleven ensures me the power to carry out the will of God. Jesus did not rely on His own strength when He left the garden. The reason He went into the garden in the first place was to get the message and the power to live the message. Step Eleven produces the same results for me.

Step Eleven has worked throughout history for all those who have made a lifetime commitment to stay in conscious contact with God. When I do Step Eleven I no longer struggle with vocation. It, like recovery, is delivered one day at a time. The promise of Step Eleven is that if I am faithful and remain in contact with God, I will always be in my new vocation.

*Your joy is your sorrow unmasked. And the selfsame well from which your laughter rises was oftentimes filled with your tears.*
*Kahlil Gibran*

## Morning Promise 11:4

*Indeed, man wishes to be happy even when he so lives as to make happiness impossible.*
*St. Augustine*

The promise of vocation is a promise that is kept on the other side of death. When I look back from my own grave, I will best view the promise of vocation. When I see my own tombstone I will come to understand vocation. Each year at Christmas two movies serve to remind me of vocation: "It's a Wonderful Life" and "A Christmas Carol." The promise of vocation in both those movies is only completely understood after the end is played out. Both George Bailey and Ebenezer Scrooge saw their lives lived to the end outside the will of God. The anguish that produced was unbearable. Yet when the characters were cast in the role of doing their vocations, doing the will of God, the future held hope and possibility. The question that faced George and Ebenezer is the same question that faces me: will I live the promise of my vocation, or won't I?

*Happiness depends upon ourselves.*
*Aristotle*

## Morning Reflection 11:4

*He that is of a merry heart hath a continual feast.*
*Bible*

Big Harold is a longshoreman. All during the Depression he fought union battles. He is a big man, 6'5", and a hard one. He drank for more than 30 years. Everybody down on the waterfront has heard about Big Harold. He is famous for his exploits.

He has a program of such spiritual quality and depth that he touches everyone he meets. He has been sober for 30-plus years. He never left the waterfront. He has had the same home group since he began his program. He chairs 12 Step meetings, serves coffee, sponsors other recovering men, and talks with newcomers. He has never joined a speakers' circult. He is nothing special in intelligence and has no particular keen political insights. He's not even someone you could call a leader. He is just like anyone else who works the Twelve Steps. He is a spiritually enlightened human being.

Harold is nearly eighty now. He gets out of his chair more slowly these days. He can't get to the number of meetings he once did, but he works his Eleventh Step faithfully. Each day he asks for knowledge of the will of God. Each day he receives the power to carry it out. Each day he decides to use the power. I expect Harold will be carrying the message until the day he drops. He will be faithful to his vocation. He will always be Big Harold to the hundreds of people he has sponsored and the thousands of men and women who have been touched by him. Harold, the big longshoreman with thirty years of recovery, will go the same route as Jesus and Mother Theresa. I imagine a moment in the not so distant future when during an Eleventh Step in Harold's own garden, he will hear it is time for him to die. I bet, at that moment, he will be talking to another drunk, carrying the message of hope, sharing his strength, telling a newcomer to let go, let God. Then in mid-sentence, Harold will simply Let Go and Let God for the last time.

*The bird of paradise alights only upon the hand that does not grasp.*
*John Berry*

# STEP TWELVE

Having had a spiritual awakening as the result of these steps, we tried to carry this message to alcoholics, and to practice these principles in all our affairs.

## Evening Prayers and Reflections for Passion

## Morning Promises and Reflections of Spirituality

## Evening Prayer 12:1

*Take heed lest passion sway thy judgment to do aught, which else free will would not admit.*
*Milton*

**O Radiant One**, something has awakened deep inside me. I feel like I am pregnant with a strange new life. I wake up in the morning and am not immediately seized by my own pain. This life inside of me stirs my heart and warms my body. I am beckoned into the morning. What is it that has come over me? My life is not different, yet it has been unmistakably changed. Somewhere, sometime, somehow my fire has been lit again; my soul once again burns with a desire to live as I have never lived before. I thank Thee for this miracle of new life. Amen.

*The duration of our passions is no more dependent on ourselves than the duration of our lives.*
*La Rochefoucauld*

## Evening Reflection 12:1

*Those who have had great passions find themselves all their lives both happy and unhappy at being cured of them.*
*La Rochefoucauld*

In Step Twelve I come full circle. Like Rip Van Winkle, I return home after a long sleep, only to find nothing looks quite the same. What has changed is not the world; it is me. My time capsule is from within. My awakening is from within. The kind of coming to life I experience is spiritual in nature. The changes produced by the Steps affect the character of my spirit. My prayer in Step Twelve is for passion.

The world before my recovery was an awful place. I hated myself. My self-esteem was nonexistent. I treated people like dogs or was treated like a dog. I wore a doormat as a coat. The world around me was a cynical, evil joke. I got along by getting even. If I couldn't get even, I pouted and pitied myself. I associated with those who had like views. My addictions got me up in the morning and put me to bed at night. Everything in my universe revolved around feeding these compulsive desires. Each new day produced new havoc; each new night produced new guilt; each new relationship died before it got started. I felt as if my passion for life and in life had been surgically removed.

Life without passion is hell on earth. Passion is to the spirit like wind to a windmill or gasoline to an engine. My addictions took my passion from me. My illness siphoned off my fuel. I howled at the moon each night for stealing my light only to shake my fist at the sun each morning for being too bright.

*In the human heart there is a ceaseless birth of passions, so that the destruction of one is almost always the establishment of another.*
*La Rochefoucauld*

## Evening Prayer 12:2

*One declaims endlessly against the passions; one imputes all of man's suffering to them. One forgets that they are also the source of all his pleasures.*
*Denis Diderot*

**O Wizard of Wizards,** I have found the ability to care. I met a stranger on the bus, an old woman. She spoke to me about her life. I found myself listening to her. I became engrossed in the story of her life. I felt no need to interrupt her and talk about my life. She shared with me her struggle with her husband's Alzheimer's disease. She allowed me to look into her soul and feel her pain. Her husband no longer recognized her, after all the years, their four children, their immigration from Finland, their struggles through the war. She is a stranger to the one she has loved and to whom she dedicated her life. She relies totally now on the love of God and the knowledge that God does have a plan for him and for her. It is with this knowledge her life is sustained. Oh, what it is to have ears that hear. Amen.

*Only passions, great passions, can elevate the soul to great things.*
*Denis Diderot*

## Evening Reflection 12:2

*Vanity plays lurid tricks with our memory, and the truth of every passion wants some pretense to make it live.*
*Joseph Conrad*

Compulsive disorders create litters of new compulsions. If I could not find passion in alcohol, I would look for it in drugs. If I could not find it in alcohol and drugs, I would run to food. No matter how bad my relationships were, I always looked for passion in sex. Each time the compulsion would take over. I would be left alone to cry by myself and wonder how God could be so cruel.

God was always the author of pain, never the mother of happiness. In my loneliness and isolation I would take fanciful journeys to different places, different times. Drunkenness became a way to conjure up the illusion of passion since I could not experience the real thing. I would lie back and dream. At night, lonely and frightened, I would close my eyes and dream about someone special lying next to me. I would transport myself out of the prison of my room and travel to some far off hideaway. In that make-believe place I would be together with someone I loved, joyous and free, full of passion for life and united in love.

The things I did in this daydream were the things I imagined successful "normal" people doing. I had children I loved who loved me. I had a job I liked. I had friends who visited me on weekends. I went to movies, plays and concerts. I was physically beautiful. I celebrated birthdays, had picnics, went to ball games and even attended Sunday church services, just like the folks in Little House on the Prairie. I imagined elaborate dances I would attend, dressed like a king. I had my beloved on my arm and we danced the night away. I came home late and made passionate love. The mornings were tender and loving. My holidays were gala events filled with family and friends. We gathered around a Thanksgiving table overflowing with food, joined hands and gave thanks for our lives.

In my dreams I was grateful for so much life, so much passion. In my fantasy world I was passionately engaged in my life's every dimension, every detail bled passion. Passion is what I cried for, what I dreamed of in my isolated moments. How different was my real world!

*Passions destroy more prejudices than philosophy does.*
*Denis Diderot*

## Evening Prayer 12:3

*We are less dissatisfied when we lack many things than when we seem to lack but one thing.*
*Eric Hoffer*

**O Wonderful Creator,** at this moment it seems that I might dare to address Thee directly. To You I owe my existence, my peace of mind, my way of life. Why is it that I find abundant life only when I give my life away? I once lived to have more: more love, more money, more things. As I would accumulate them I would invariably feel empty and alone. Now my world has turned upside down. To give is to get, to get is to give. The less I want, the more I have. The less I expect, the greater the abundance. Thank you for showing me how to live. Amen.

*Often, the thing we pursue most passionately is but a substitute for the one thing we really want and cannot have.*
*Eric Hoffer*

## Evening Reflection 12:3

*The mind is the soul's eye, not its source of power. That lies in the heart, in other words, in the passions.*
*Vauvenargues*

The one burning realization in my twilight dream world was there were no expectations. The evil monster that snatched me away from my life was locked away somewhere. There was no drunken fight at the dinner table. There was no drunken, jealous tirade at a dance because a friend glanced with affection at my girl. There was no waking up to the face of a bleary-eyed stranger I had brought home to my bed because I could not stand one more night alone. There were no family gatherings where all the nieces and nephews fled from me because I reeked of alcohol or looked crazy from drugs. In my dreams, there were no late night visits to the refrigerator where I gorged myself into tears.

These dark, horrible addictions were taken away in my dreams. I never felt the agony of being abandoned yet one more time by one more loved one. I never felt the numbing, emotionless wound of having to dress for battle each morning. In these dreams I lived a life without disease, without addiction, without compulsions. I was healthy.

In my real world, I did live with disease, with addiction, with compulsions. There were no baseball games, walks in the park, loving dinners, joyful children, quiet nights at home, meaningful work, stable friendships, a faithful marriage. There was only passionless dreadful misery. This was the world I awoke to day after day, until I stared Death in the face and found myself contemplating suicide. My fear was no longer dying; it was continuing to live. Death would be preferable to a passionless existence.

As I was about to write the final word in the book of my life, I was introduced to Twelve Step Recovery. Everything became possible.

*It would not be better if things happened to men just as they wish.*
*Heraclitus*

## Evening Prayer 12:4

*Men have a thousand desires to a bushel of choices.*
*Henry Ward Beecher*

**O Thou Whom I Call Mother And Father And Friend**, I have formed a bond with You as consuming as any I can imagine. I realize there is no life outside my relationship with You. Why I had to try every other possible option before I turned to You, I can't say. When I knew You had the power over my life, I fought long and hard before I turned my will and life over to You. I held out the hope that maybe I was Godlike. After many years, all hope was washed away; any faith in myself was destroyed; and I was left with a feeling of desolate emptiness. Now I have found a deep love for this Power over my life. I rely on this Power, I worship this Force and embrace it as my God. Amen.

*If you desire many things, many things will seem but a few.*
*Benjamin Franklin*

## Evening Reflection 12:4

*Those desires that do not bring pain if they are not satisfied are not necessary; and they are easily thrust aside whenever to satisfy them appears difficult or likely to cause injury.*
*Epicurus*

I run directly into the passion of the Twelfth Step. I am a beneficiary of the spiritual awakening of someone else who has taken the journey through the Twelve Steps. That someone came to me like a guardian angel, a living, breathing example of the Twelve Steps and recovery.

The Twelfth Step is passion. It is being filled with life that feeds off of giving life. The phrase, "you can't keep it if you don't give it away," speaks directly to the issue. You can't have passion if you don't live with passion. One recovery begets another recovery. The Twelve Steps allow me to live my awakening moment by moment, to live to carry the revelation of life after death to anyone who will hear. The reward for carrying the message is new fuel for more life, more passion, more work.

*We are never further from our wishes than when we imagine that we possess what we have desired.*
*Andre Gide*

## Morning Promise 12:1

*Many persons have a wrong idea of what constitutes true happiness. It is not attained through self-gratification but through fidelity to a worthy purpose.*
*Helen Keller*

Spirituality is a promise of walking forever with God. This is not as lofty as it sounds. When I walk with God I walk with whom God walks. I find that as I walk, people will walk along with me. Those who embrace the promise of spirituality affect everyone they meet. They repel evil and people that seek to do them harm. They attract good people and all manner of positive forces. Spirituality is following the light. The promise is that I will be able to distinguish light from dark, day from night. Spiritual people know they don't own their spirituality; they only borrow the light from God. I take on the characteristics of holiness because I am surrounded by holiness. I am spiritual because of my freely chosen association. The promise of spirituality is a promise granted each moment I decide to continue my walk in Paradise.

*Obstacles cannot crush me. Every obstacle yields to stern resolve. He who is fixed to a star does not change his mind.*
*Leonardo Da Vinci*

## Morning Reflection 12:1

*A windmill is eternally at work to accomplish one end, although it shifts with every variation of the weathercock, and assumes ten different position in a day.*
*Charles Caleb Colton*

The dark night of the soul is finally over in Step 12. Spiritual awakening is a dream come true. I am living in a world in which I thought only a chosen few could live. The idyllic never-never land of my daydreams has become a realistic always-always land. I can either have true love with real problems, or I can have teary-eyed Thanksgivings with dry turkey. I can have a Saturday dance with slippers that do not fit. I can have babies that cry at 3:00 a.m. I can have a mother and father who die. All this I can have without killing myself. I need not condition my joy because I no longer condition my life on alcohol. I have things in life that are paradoxical without running in fear. People are born; people die. I am happy; I am sad; I was young; I am old. There is night, day, winter, summer. These are all acceptable realities to me. My life is immersed in acceptance; it is the answer.

"And acceptance is the answer to all my problems today. When I am disturbed, it is because I find some person, place, thing, or situation - some fact of my life - unacceptable to me, and now I can find no serenity until I accept that person, place, thing, or situation as being exactly the way it is supposed to be at this moment. Nothing, absolutely nothing happens in God's world by mistake. Until I could accept my alcoholism, I could not stay sober; unless I accept life completely on life's terms, I cannot be happy. I need to concentrate not so much on what needs to be changed in the world as on what needs to be changed in me and in my attitudes."

*Alcoholics Anonymous*, p.449

*Good purposes should be the directors of good actions, not the apology for bad.*
*Thomas Fuller*

## Morning Promise 12:2

*Let us not be weary in well doing: for in due season we shall reap, if we faint not.*
*Bible*

The promise of spirituality is like a butterfly emerging from a cocoon. The cocoon is the protection I receive from my other Steps. The Twelfth Step is like f'ying like a butterfly. I wonder how it is this ugly old larva could emerge as a beautiful butterfly; there must be some trick. My first response is to deny I have seen it. There must have been a butterfly perched behind the cocoon. My second response is to believe, but only in a qualified way; if that larva is a butterfly, it must be a special kind of larva. The promise of spirituality is unequivocal. If I dare to work a program, I will emerge a person of profound spirituality, just as a butterfly emerges winged and beautiful from a larva's cocoon.

*If I am virtuous and worthy, for whom should I not maintain a proper concern?*
*Confucius*

## Morning Reflection 12:2

*A man of humanity is one who, in seeking to establish himself, finds a foothold for others and who, desiring attainment for himself, helps others to attain.*
*Confucius*

Spirituality as the promise in the Twelfth Step has certain definable characteristics. Where there once was fear, there now exists trust; where there once was self-pity, there now is gratitude; where there once was resentment, there now is acceptance; where there once was dishonesty, there now is honesty. Spirituality is not a state of mind; it is a state of being. Recovery is not a physical characteristic; it is a spiritual characteristic.

There is no need to leave the plane of reality to find spirituality. It is much more than participating in a rudimentary life process. I become part of the life cycle, part of the ongoing living, dying and regeneration process. God has never had a bias against dying, only man does. God does not think death is man's punishment for living. Death is as much a part of living as birth. I see in my 12th Step work how one man's fodder is another man's fertilizer. The muscle of life shows every time I dare to share with another person my strength, hope and experience with my addiction. When I am rigorously honest and truthfully relate how it was for me and how it came to be after I worked the Steps, I see the illuminating light of recognition.

When the great and powerful Wizard of Oz quit pretending that his life was full of big deals and shared what he really knew about life, the light went on with Dorothy and the gang. The Tin Man realized he had had a heart all along. The Lion realized he had had courage all along. The Scarecrow realized he had had a brain all along. The Wizard was not a wizard, he was a man who stayed close to the program. When he stayed close, he revealed deep spirituality. When he was caught up in his wizard role, he was a foolish carnival huckster. The difference between a wizard and a sponsor is trust. A wizard depends on smoke, mirrors, and a lot of bluff to make his point. A sponsor takes great pains not to divert one inch from the truth.

Twelve Step spirituality requires sponsorship. There is no way to practice spirituality except to practice common principles. I must be ever vigilant to focus on the way I incorporate principles into my life. My own vitality requires that I work with others in recovery. My mission in life is not so much recovery as it is manifesting God's will. I know that God's will for me is that I stay in recovery, so recovery as the will of God becomes apparent for me when I work with those who have not yet heard the message.

*In abstract love of humanity one almost always only loves oneself.*
*Dostoevsky*

## Morning Promise 12:3

*All fortune belongs to him who has a contented mind. Is not the whole earth covered with leather for him whose feet are encased in shoes?*
*Panchatantra*

A promise of spirituality is like no other promise. It is not a retreat from life, but a route into life. I have come to the point where I no longer rely on the world for my identity or my fellow man for my recognition. I find everything worth having, everything worth knowing, and everything worth being entirely contained within my relationship with God. The promise of spirituality means I can be nothing else when I embrace the promise of this relationship. What does a spiritual person look like? Much like any person who has been taught a great lesson in life, who has been beaten, who has lost much. A spiritual person knows the humility that comes from being thrown a life preserver in a stormy sea.

*If thou covetest riches, ask not but for contentment, which is an immense treasure.*
*Sa'di*

## Morning Reflection 12:3

*That man is happiest who lives from day to day and asks no more, garnering the simple goodness of a life.*
*Euripides*

When I practice the 12 Steps in all my affairs, I live the resurrection. I identify with those who have experienced life after death. The resurrected person knows death has no claim on their soul. There is nothing left to fear.

The spirit that breathes through me is like a hot wind. I now know what Paul experienced when he was knocked off his horse on the road to Damascus. I am not intimidated by the lives of great people; I have joined the select group of people saved so others might be saved.

When I heard such words in the past, I backed away because they sounded so strange and foreign. I ridiculed those who spoke of being born again as fools and followers of fools. Now I have my own experience to prove the point. I have the irrefutable truth that the lame can walk, the deaf hear, the dumb speak, because I walk, hear and speak. I can name places, provide evidence, present witnesses. One need not depend on logic to embrace the truth in what I say. When I tell the truth about my life, those who are still suffering begin to wonder, "Could this become me?"

When I remember my assault in Washington D.C. I remember hitting bottom and bouncing off the floor. What drove me to that despair seems like such a small event. Armed with a belief in a Higher Power there are no more Big Deals.

Because my priorities have changed, new areas of my life take on value. I get my sustenance in life from my conscious contact with God, nothing else.

> God grant me the serenity to accept the
> things I cannot change, the courage to
> change the things I can and the wisdom
> to know the difference.

*Fat hens lay few eggs.*
*German Proverb*

## Morning Promise 12:4

*He who would make serious use of his life must always act as though he had a long time to live and must schedule his time as though he were about to die.*
*Emile Littre*

The promise of spirituality is like a perpetually full bank account. All our relationships will ultimately be defined by this state of being. I walk as one who has been resurrected from the dead. I do not know if a person who has not experienced a kind of death can achieve spirituality. I do know that spirituality has everything to do with life. I see men and women who were once dead in every meaningful sense now walking with a life and vitality truly miraculous. People in recovery are resurrected people of the spirit. There is a wind that blows over them. You know them by their feel, by their uncanny sixth sense. They seem to understand the mysteries of life. They appear to be "on the way" or maybe "of the way."

*The great and glorious masterpiece of man is to know how to live to purpose.*
*Montaigne*

## Morning Reflection 12:4

*I have learned, in whatsoever state I am, therewith to be content.*
*Bible*

Finally, the promise for the 12th Step is for spirituality. I find the promise fulfilled in working with other people. There is no hint of pious detachment; whatever I do, I ultimately do for myself. Every time I carry the message and rely on God's strength to stay recovered, I win. Twelve Step spirituality is bound to the First Step. It does not point to the end of the journey; it points to the beginning. When Dorothy clicked her heels three times and said, "I want to go home," she was transported right back to Kansas. She made no stops in Nebraska or New York City. So it is with the 12 Steps. After I am awakened, I return to share my awakening with others.

I have asked myself on many occasions, "How are things different for me? How have the 12 Steps changed my life? How have I changed?" I guess I don't change; I just stay connected. If I had to relive the scene in that hospital in Washington, I think it would go something like this:

I would look up at the priest with a big smile. I would wink at him three times -- one, two, three. Then I would say, "I want to go home, I want to go home, I want to go home."

*Do not spoil what you have by desiring what you have not; but remember that what you now have was once among the things only hoped for.*
*Epicurus*